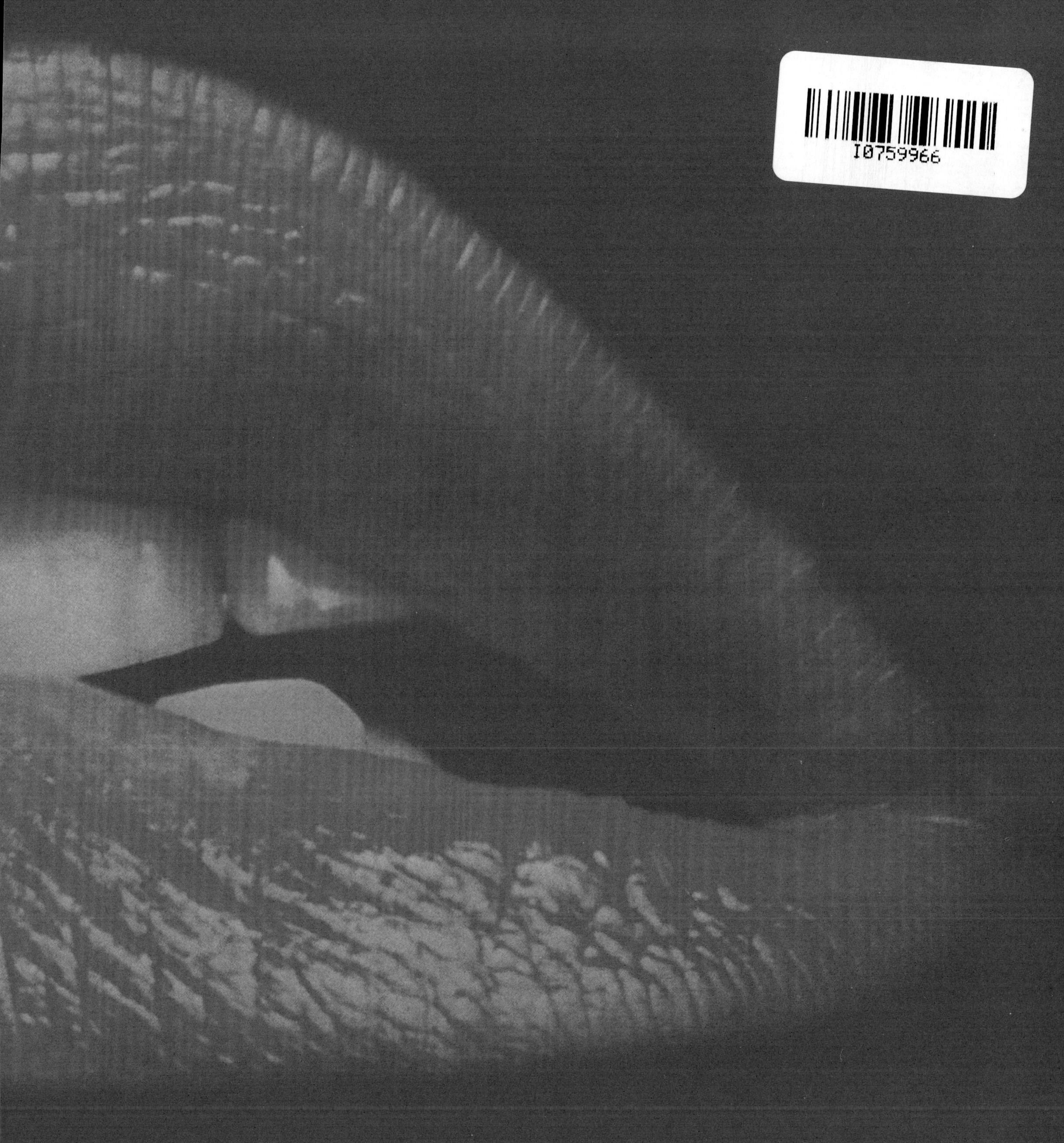

IT WAS GREAT WHEN
IT ALL BEGAN

IT WAS GREAT WHEN IT ALL BEGAN

THE ORIGINAL
ROCKY HORROR SHOW
ANNOTATED SCRIPT

MALCOLM CROFT
FOREWORD BY RICHARD O'BRIEN

weldon**owen**

THE ROYAL COURT THEATRE UPSTAIRS
PRESENTS ...
THE ROCKY HORROR SHOW
BY RICHARD O'BRIEN
SOMETHING FOR EVERYONE
THRILLS CHILLS AND SPILLS
Eddie
BRAD AND JANET FOUND IT WAS A NIGHT THEY WERE TO REMEMBER FOR A VERY LONG TIME

Original 1973 London playbill.

INTRODUCTION

Imagine the scene. It's June 19, 1973, 10:30 p.m. Thunder erupts and lightning strikes. The city of London's dark skies are illuminated in bright forked light as huge storms drench the capital's roads below, as well as any late-night revelers who dare walk the rain-soaked streets.

A cast of first-time performers prepares to take the stage for a new play—a rock and roll musical—written by an unknown, unemployed actor: Richard O'Brien. For Richard, getting his erotic nightmare (set to music) this far had already been a strange journey. But he didn't know that this fateful opening night would be the first step in changing his world forever.

As the Royal Court Theatre Upstairs drew back its curtain—despite its stage being so small there wasn't even a curtain—all eyes were on Richard and his misfit crew. When the legendary horror actor (and Richard's idol) Vincent Price took to his seat, thunder struck again. As the lightning flashed, it eerily illuminated Price's face in the dark, squashed confines of the tiny theater.

"Fuck me!" Richard exclaimed joyfully. "That's a good omen."

Indeed, it was. In that frightening storm, *The Rocky Horror Sho*w was born. It was a raging success.

The lightning bolt struck again nine months later, in March 1974, when *The Rocky Horror Show* was reborn–not for the last time—at Los Angeles's Roxy Theatre. There, too, it became the toast of Tinseltown, proving once and for all it was no longer just an experimental fringe production for cultural outcasts. (Though they did also turn up in abundance, naturally.) Similar to Rocky himself, the show had grown up into something beyond handsome and muscular–it was an electrifying phenomenon! As if to prove it, many of world's most influential artists—John Lennon, Mick Jagger, Jack Nicholson, Anjelica Huston, Cher, and Elvis Presley—flocked to the Roxy to bathe in Rocky's freshly squeezed juices.

More than fifty years later, the stage show (and its iconic film adaptation) is still very much "a mental mind fuck," to quote Frank-N-Furter. *The Rocky Horror Show* is still performed on stages all over the world and continues to inspire, influence, and entertain millions, regenerating with each new generation. The creature, and the legend, lives on.

Ladies and gentlemen—and everyone in between—welcome to *It Was Great When It All Began: The Original Rocky Horror Show Annotated Script*, the official celebration of the stage version of Richard O'Brien's rock and roll horror creation. Inside you'll find the original Royal Court theatrical script in its entirety, including song lyrics, accompanied by a feast of photographs taken during the original Royal Court and Roxy performances (one easy way to tell the difference—Tim Curry has blond hair in the London show; producer Lou Adler had him dye his hair black for the LA staging). As an extra-special bonus, and completely free of charge, the script is annotated with the most classic audience callouts and participation, something that began at New York's Waverly Theater in April 1977 and is now also done at every live stage performance. As you read, feel free to shout them out as loud as you like. We'll be listening.

Right, enough with the foreplay—it's time to give yourself over to absolute pleasure . . .

Tim Curry (Frank-N-Furter), Abigale Haness (Janet), and Bill Miller (Brad), Los Angeles cast.

DISASTER
ICA
4 July -
12 August
RICHARD O'BRIEN'S
ROGET'S
THESAURUS

A BRIEF REFLECTION UPON THE WINNING OF THE ROCKY HORROR SHOW

by Richard O'Brien

Rocky Horror has enjoyed an audience of interactive theatergoers for many years now, and consequently this tends to encourage many productions and actors to play up to and for these audiences. Their (the actors') playing style becomes broader and coarser, and before we know it, much of the wit and understated subtext get lost.

Only two players are allowed to "interact" with the audience, and they are the Narrator and Frank-N-Furter, and even they must be guided by wit and intelligence and understand that less, very often, means more, and like all others must remain loyal to the narrative and their stereotypical character's needs. Remember that when played "seriously," the play becomes funnier.

Key scenes:

1. The car journey is the beginning of our odyssey—"Over at the Frankenstein Place" should not be played at a fast tempo but should be full of mystery and portent.
2. The arrival of Riff Raff at the door (Scene Two).
   (Q) Why does he invite Brad & Janet in?
   (A) Because in his scheming mind he thinks that they might somehow or other upset Frank's applecart.
3. Unmind a lock (Scene Four). This speech is what I refer to as "Fortune Cookie philosophy." Frank should REALLY flirt with both Brad and Janet and not make them his dupes. At this stage, he should be charm personified. He is thrilled at having a NEW audience.
4. When Frank tells Magenta that he is indeed grateful to both her and her little brother, Riff Raff (Scene Nine), she must not show her anger but rather her smile. Likewise, Riff must play the cringing cur until Frank turns away—THEN we MUST see the worm turn.

Before I give a short rundown on characterization, I must stress that there should be NO touching, fondling, or looking up skirts or down knickers at ANY TIME other than the bedroom scenes by ANYONE. We have nowhere to go once we have. Keep the sexual tension in a constant state of foreplay—to travel hopefully is better than to arrive.

Richard O'Brien and Richard Hartley.

Frank-N-Furter

Part Eisenstein's *Ivan the Terrible* (1944)
Part Cruella de Vil
Part Dracula
Part Casanova
Part Samurai Warrior

He is intelligent, charming, ruthless, and vain. He is NOT camp in the effete way. He could turn up in Noh theater, Kabuki, Berkoff, expressionistic theater, and even ballet. His intentions must be perceived, every move, every action, every word delivered to further his needs. Stillness is of the essence—strength rather than fluff. Allow the power to burn like a searchlight from the solar plexus—sweeping through the audience and embracing them and the other players. Avoid becoming a poor drag act.

Horses for Courses: Tim Curry * Alan Rickman * Freddy Mercury * Marilyn Manson * Vincent Price * Klaus Kinski * Larry Olivier

Riff Raff

A cliché IGOR figure—sneaky, jealous of Frank's charm, duplicitous, and self-pitying. His lust for his sister is driven by his need to control. He is scheming, clever, and mean-spirited. We must see the wheels turning.

Horses for Courses: Peter Lorre * Robert Helpmann * Nosferatu * Lon Chaney

Magenta

She is a watcher, a very dark horse, a voyeur. She feeds off just being there. She is indifferent to Riff's obsessional love for her. He amuses her, as do most people and things. She is a Gormenghast figure—a black widow spider. She has a secret, a private joke, and she's not about to share it with us as we are very likely its subject matter.

Horses for Courses: Simone Signoret * Juliette Gréco * Jeanne Moreau * Lucrezia Borgia

Columbia

A half-smart, streetwise flake. She's not going to age well. She'd make a great guest on an American trailer trash talk show. These days she might even get a show of her own. She's been around the block a time or three. She's lovable, vulnerable, and loyal in the way women who "stand by their man" are.

Horses for Courses: Lots of present-day pop tarts * Courtney Love * Mamie Van Doren * Lili St. Cyr * Lil' Kim

Brad

Wooden leading man, patronizing and stiff with responsibility—misogyny masks his latent fear of emasculation.

Horses for Courses: The covers of knitting magazines * B movies * '60s jocksville

Janet

The girl next door with a need to be married so that she can further sublimate her true inner needs. At the start of the show, she has bought into the idea of her role in society, but at the end, Brad the hunter has become a wounded dinosaur and his mate has woken from her self-imposed dream.

Horses for Courses: Romance comics * Roy Lichtenstein paintings

Eddie/Dr. Scott

Eddie takes care of himself (herself, in the NY Production). Dr. Scott is, once again, another stereotypical character. The mad professor—the government "research" scientist. He should NOT use a German accent except, perhaps, at moments for comedy.

Horses for Courses: Henry Kissinger * Dr. Strangelove * Wernher von Braun * Stephen Hawking

CAST OF CHARACTERS

Dr. Frank-N-Furter, a Scientist
Riff Raff, a Handyman
Janet Weiss, a Heroine
Brad Majors, a Hero
Magenta, a Domestic
Columbia, a Groupie
Rocky Horror, a Creation
Eddie, an Ex-Delivery Boy
Dr. Everett Scott, a Rival Scientist
The Narrator
The Transylvanians

THE SONGS

"Science Fiction/Double Feature" — Usherette, Phantoms

"Dammit Janet" — Brad, Janet, Phantoms

"Over at the Frankenstein Place" — Janet, Brad, Riff Raff, Phantoms

"Sweet Transvestite" — Frank-N-Furter, Brad, Riff Raff, Magenta, Columbia, Phantoms

"The Time Warp" — Riff Raff, Magenta, Columbia, Phantoms

"The Sword of Damocles" — Rocky, Narrator, Ensemble

"I Can Make You a Man" — Frank-N-Furter, Ensemble

"Hot Patootie (Bless My Soul)" — Eddie, Ensemble

"I Can Make You a Man (Reprise)" — Dr. Frank-N-Furter, Janet, Ensemble

"Touch-A, Touch-A, Touch Me" — Janet, Magenta, Columbia

"Once in a While" — Brad, Narrator, Phantoms

"Eddie's Teddy" — Dr. Scott, Narrator, Columbia, Ensemble

"Wise Up Janet Weiss" — Frank-N-Furter, Narrator, Janet, Magenta, Ensemble

"Rose Tint My World" — Columbia, Rocky, Brad, Janet, Riff Raff, Frank-N-Furter, Dr. Scott

"I'm Going Home" — Frank-N-Furter, Ensemble

"Super Heroes" — Brad, Janet, Narrator, Phantoms

"Science Fiction/Double Feature (Reprise)" — Usherette, Phantoms

ORIGINAL CASTS

Patricia Quinn as Usherette/Magenta

Julie Covington as Janet Weiss

Christopher Malcolm as Brad Majors

Nell Campbell as Columbia

Tim Curry as Frank-N-Furter

LONDON 1973

The Rocky Horror Show was first performed at the Theatre Upstairs, Royal Court Theatre, London. The first preview was on June 17, 1973, and the production opened two days later on June 19. The performance was directed by Jim Sharman, with set design by Brian Thomson, costume design by Sue Blane, and arrangements by Richard Hartley.

Jonathan Adams as Narrator

Richard O'Brien as Riff Raff

Rayner Bourton as Rocky

Paddy O'Hagan as Eddie/Dr. Scott

Jamie Donnelly as Magenta/Usherette

Abigale Haness as Janet Weiss

Bill Miller as Brad Majors

Tim Curry as Frank-N-Furter

Boni Enten as Columbia

LOS ANGELES 1974

The Rocky Horror Show had its US premiere at the Roxy Theatre in Los Angeles on March 24, 1974. Called the original Roxy cast, this performance was also directed by Jim Sharman. Tim Curry is the only member from the original London cast.

Graham Jarvis as Narrator

Bruce Scott as Riff Raff

Kim Milford as Rocky Horror

Meat Loaf as Eddie/Dr. Scott

Coca-Cola
ACME

Production Note:

SETTING THE SCENE

The setting is a single-level movie theater, once opulent, now on the verge of being condemned, in a seedy area. The dilapidated facade is papered with half-torn Rocky Horror *posters. The lobby is papered with old horror movie posters, a jukebox, and pinball machines. "Apologies for the inconvenience" signs due to the impending demolition are plastered throughout.*

Inside the auditorium, the room is very dimly lit, and what can be seen is decaying, cracked, or missing. A lifeless arm can be seen hanging through a large crack in the ceiling's plasterwork, and collapsed chairs are stacked under the scaffolding. For all appearances, this is a room mid-demolition. A string of bare bulbs runs from a front corner to the opposite rear corner. The entire interior is covered in dark-blue canvas, stenciled with ACME Demolition Co.

The audience faces a proscenium and red velvet curtains. Scaffolding runs along both side walls, finishing at raised platforms on either side of the stage. The stage-right scaffold has a ladder running from the stage to the platform, where an old Coca-Cola chest-style fridge is sitting in front of a black curtain. The center aisle is blocked by a catwalk running from one of the back doors to the center of the stage. The stage-left scaffold is also accessed by a ladder; on the platform is the laboratory set, consisting of a hospital gurney with neon tubes in rows behind it, as well as test tubes and chemical flasks filled with colored liquids arranged in front. The lab set is hidden behind a torn and stained curtain resembling a painter's drop cloth.

The band performs from behind the movie screen, which is gauze, fine enough to see through when lit from behind.

The set at the Roxy, Los Angeles.

"THE ROCKY HORROR SHOW"

by

Richard O'Brien

Royal Court Theatre,
Sloane Square,
London S.W.1.

Tel: 01-730-5174

PROLOGUE

(RIFF RAFF, COLUMBIA, and EDDIE/DR. SCOTT dressed as USHERS in moth-eaten suits and clear plastic face masks enter the theater and menace patrons by standing and staring at them, or sitting in a empty seat next to them until they notice and yelp with fright. At one point one usher begins vacuuming the carpet. The band slips in and takes their places.)
(The USHERS approach the stage, as the lights dim. There is a scream and the curtains open to reveal an USHERETTE carrying a candy tray, sitting on a black square block in the center of the stage, with the cinema screen behind her. She is covered with white gauze, lit only by the flashlight from her candy tray.
The three USHERS move toward her.

USHERS (*to the audience*)
Glad you could COME tonight!

(They remove the USHERETTE's veil, a spotlight hits the USHERETTE and she stands to sing.

Patricia Quinn: I began the show sitting onstage with my ice cream tray under a piece of netting. The audience would come in and poke at the netting, trying to figure out what it was.

Original script cover page, 1973.

SCIENCE FICTION/ DOUBLE FEATURE

USHERETTE

MICHAEL RENNIE WAS ILL
THE DAY THE EARTH STOOD STILL
BUT HE TOLD US WHERE WE STAND
AND FLASH GORDON WAS THERE
IN SILVER UNDERWEAR
CLAUDE RAINS WAS THE INVISIBLE MAN
THEN SOMETHING WENT WRONG
FOR FAY WRAY AND KING KONG
THEY GOT CAUGHT IN A CELLULOID JAM
THEN AT A DEADLY PACE
IT CAME FROM OUTER SPACE
AND THIS IS HOW THE MESSAGE RAN.

(CHORUS)
(PHANTOMS DO THE OOHHS ETC.)
SCIENCE FICTION—DOUBLE FEATURE
DR. X WILL BUILD A CREATURE
SEE ANDROIDS FIGHTING BRAD AND JANET
ANNE FRANCES STARS IN FORBIDDEN PLANET
OH—AT THE LATE NIGHT
DOUBLE FEATURE
PICTURE SHOW.

I KNEW LEO G. CARROL
WAS OVER A BARREL
WHEN TARANTULA TOOK TO THE HILLS
AND I REALLY GOT HOT
WHEN I SAW JANETTE SCOTT
FIGHT A TRIFFID THAT SPITS POISON AND KILLS
DANA ANDREWS SAID PRUNES
GIVE HIM THE RHUNES
AND PASSING THEM USED LOTS OF SKILLS
AND WHEN WORLD'S COLLIDE
SAID GEORGE PAL TO HIS BRIDE
I'M GOING TO GIVE YOU SOME TERRIBLE THRILLS
LIKE A—

(CHORUS)
SCIENCE FICTION—DOUBLE FEATURE
DR. X WILL BUILD A CREATURE
SEE ANDROIDS FIGHTING BRAD AND JANET
ANNE FRANCES STARS IN FORBIDDEN PLANET
OH—AT THE LATE NIGHT DOUBLE FEATURE
PICTURE SHOW.
I WANT TO GO
OH—AT THE LATE NIGHT
DOUBLE FEATURE
PICTURE SHOW
BY R.K.O.
OH—AT THE LATE NIGHT
DOUBLE FEATURE
PICTURE SHOW
IN THE BACK ROW
OH—AT THE LATE NIGHT
DOUBLE FEATURE
PICTURE SHOW.

Patricia Quinn (Usherette/Magenta), London cast.

Sloane
CINEMAS
STRAWBERRY
TIME

SCENE ONE

(The piano plays the sound of wedding bells. BRAD and JANET run onstage, breathless, JANET carrying a bouquet, as the Lights come up. The PHANTOMS throw confetti over them, then climb to the platforms to sing in the next song.)

JANET

Oh Brad, wasn't it wonderful—didn't Betty look radiantly beautiful—I can't believe it—just an hour ago she was plain Betty Munroe and now she's Mrs. Ralf Hapshatt.

BRAD

Yes, Janet—Ralf's a lucky guy.

JANET

Yes.

BRAD

Everyone knows Betty's a wonderful little cook.

JANET

Yes.

BRAD

And Ralf himself will be in line for promotion in a year or two.

JANET

Yes, Brad.

(BRAD takes the microphone.)

Julie Covington (Janet) and Christopher Malcolm (Brad), London cast.

DAMMIT JANET

BRAD

HEY, JANET.

JANET

YES BRAD.

BRAD

I'VE GOT SOMETHING TO SAY.

JANET

YES.

BRAD

I REALLY LOVED THE SKILLFUL WAY
YOU BEAT THE OTHER GIRLS TO
THE BRIDE'S BOUQUET.

	PHANTOMS
THE RIVER WAS DEEP BUT I SWAM IT.	Janet
THE FUTURE IS OURS SO LET'S PLAN IT.	Janet
SO PLEASE DON'T TELL ME TO CAN IT.	Janet
I'VE ONE THING TO SAY AND THAT'S . . .	
DAMN IT—JANET—I LOVE YOU.	
THE ROAD WAS LONG BUT I RAN IT.	Janet
THERE'S A FIRE IN MY HEART AND YOU FAN IT.	Janet
IF THERE'S A FOOL FOR YOU THEN I AM IT.	Janet
I'VE ONE THING TO SAY AND THAT'S	
DAMN IT—JANET—I LOVE YOU.	

HERE'S A RING TO PROVE I'M NO JOKER
(Bell voices.)
THERE'S THREE WAYS THAT LOVE CAN GROW
THAT'S GOOD—BAD—OR MEDIOCRE
J-A-N-E-T
I LOVE YOU SO.
(JANET admires the ring, throws the bouquet into the wings and grabs the microphone.)

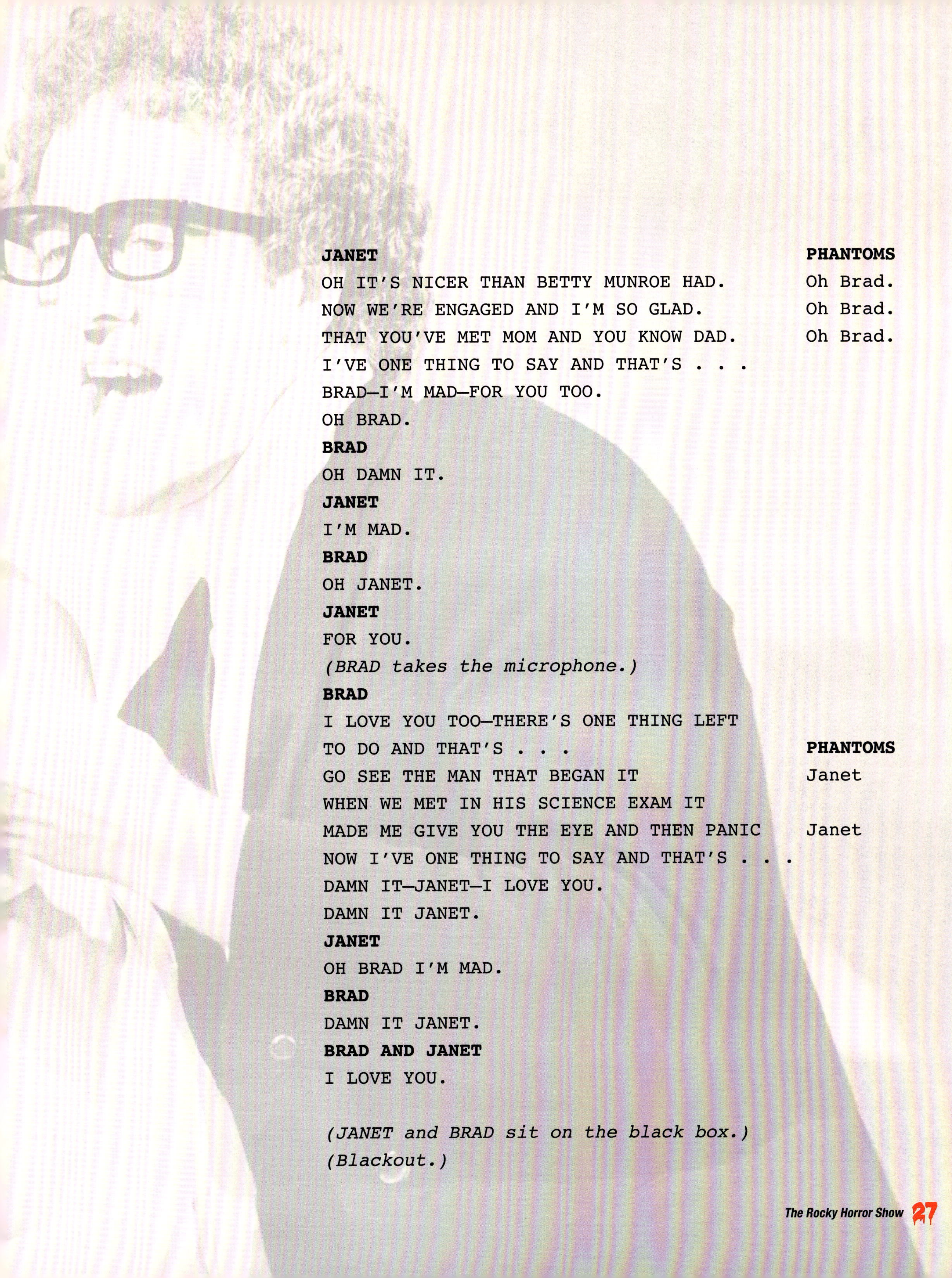

JANET | **PHANTOMS**

OH IT'S NICER THAN BETTY MUNROE HAD. Oh Brad.
NOW WE'RE ENGAGED AND I'M SO GLAD. Oh Brad.
THAT YOU'VE MET MOM AND YOU KNOW DAD. Oh Brad.
I'VE ONE THING TO SAY AND THAT'S . . .
BRAD—I'M MAD—FOR YOU TOO.
OH BRAD.

BRAD

OH DAMN IT.

JANET

I'M MAD.

BRAD

OH JANET.

JANET

FOR YOU.

(BRAD takes the microphone.)

BRAD

I LOVE YOU TOO—THERE'S ONE THING LEFT
TO DO AND THAT'S . . . **PHANTOMS**
GO SEE THE MAN THAT BEGAN IT Janet
WHEN WE MET IN HIS SCIENCE EXAM IT
MADE ME GIVE YOU THE EYE AND THEN PANIC Janet
NOW I'VE ONE THING TO SAY AND THAT'S . . .
DAMN IT—JANET—I LOVE YOU.
DAMN IT JANET.

JANET

OH BRAD I'M MAD.

BRAD

DAMN IT JANET.

BRAD AND JANET

I LOVE YOU.

(JANET and BRAD sit on the black box.)
(Blackout.)

THE ROCKY HORROR SHOW

(Spotlight picks up the NARRATOR, who is sitting in the front row. He walks up onto the stage, and with his back turned to the audience, opens a secret door in the proscenium. He makes a creaking sound as he slowly opens the door. Inside are shelves. On one shelf is a large book. He takes the book and turns to the audience, blowing a cloud of dust from the book over the front row.)

NARRATOR

I would like—if I may—to
take you on a strange journey.
(He opens the book and starts to read)
It seemed a fairly
ordinary night when Brad Majors,
and his fiancée Janet Weiss . . .
left Denton that late November evening to
visit a Dr. Evrett Scott
ex tutor and now friend to both of them . . .
Its true there were dark storm clouds,
heavy—black and pendulous—toward
which they were—driving,
its true also that the spare tire they were
carrying was badly in need of some air—
but they being normal kids
and on a night out—well—they were not going to let
a storm spoil the events of their evening.
On a night out.
(Thunder) **It was a night out**
they were to remember
(Thunder) **for a very . . . long . . . time.**
(Blackout)

Jonathan Adams (Narrator), London cast.

SCENE TWO

(A spotlight picks up BRAD and JANET sitting on the box, miming being in a car. BRAD is driving with his left hand, while his right hand is imitating a windshield wiper. JANET's left hand lies across her like a seat belt and her right arm is also imitating a windshield wiper. The USHERS make the sound of the car. It is a stormy night, and flashes of lightning are seen. The car stops.)

BRAD

Hmmm.

JANET

What's the matter, Brad darling?

BRAD

I think we took the wrong fork a
few miles back there.
We'd better go on ahead up the road and see
if we can find our way back.

(JANET and BRAD "drive" down center stage and stop on the edge of the stage. The PHANTOMS mimic a tire blow-out. BRAD and JANET sway as if BRAD slammed on the brakes.)

Oh darn! Janet.

JANET

What was that bang?

(THEY out of the car.)

BRAD

We seem to have a blow-out in the front left-hand tire.

JANET

Oh . . .

(Pause. Lightning and thunder.)

BRAD

You'd better stay here and keep warm while I go for help.

JANET

But where will you go? We're in the middle of nowhere.

BRAD

Didn't we pass a castle back down the road a few miles? Maybe they have a telephone I might use.

JANET

I'm coming with you.

BRAD

There's no point in both of us getting wet.

(RIFF RAFF makes his way to a ladder and climbs it.)

JANET

I'm coming with you. Besides, darling, the owner of the phone may be a beautiful woman, and you may never come back.

BRAD

Ha Ha Ha.

(PHANTOMS take up the laughter—They exit with car.)

(JANET picks up the microphone.)

Belinda Sinclair: During rehearsals, I definitely invented the windscreen wiper. They have a car onstage now, but we never had one, so I became the windscreen wiper.

OVER AT THE FRANKENSTEIN PLACE

JANET
IN THE VELVET DARKNESS
OF THE BLACKEST NIGHT
BURNING BRIGHT—THERE'S A GUIDING STAR
NO MATTER WHAT OR WHO YOU ARE.
BRAD & JANET
THERE'S A LIGHT
PHANTOMS
OVER AT THE FRANKENSTEIN PLACE
BRAD & JANET
THERE'S A LIGHT
PHANTOMS
BURNING IN THE FIREPLACE
JANET
THERE'S A LIGHT . . . LIGHT IN THE
DARKNESS OF EVERYBODY'S LIFE
(BRAD climbs a ladder half-way to the laboratory, and points upward.)
BRAD
I CAN SEE THE FLAG FLY
I CAN SEE THE RAIN
JUST THE SAME—THERE HAS GOT TO BE
SOMETHING BETTER HERE—FOR YOU AND ME.
(BRAD climbs down.)
BRAD & JANET
THERE'S A LIGHT
PHANTOMS
OVER AT THE FRANKENSTEIN PLACE
BRAD & JANET
THERE'S A LIGHT
PHANTOMS
BURNING IN THE FIREPLACE
BRAD
THERE'S A LIGHT . . . LIGHT IN THE
DARKNESS OF EVERYBODY'S LIFE
(A light pin spots RIFF RAFF.) The sound of his voice causes BRAD and JANET to each run to opposite sides of the stage.)
RIFF RAFF
THE DARKNESS MUST GO DOWN THE RIVER
OF NIGHTS DREAMING FLOW MORPHIA SLOW
LET THE SUN AND LIGHT COME STREAMING
INTO MY LIFE INTO MY LIFE
(The light fades on RIFF RAFF. JANET and BRAD return to each other.)
JANET & BRAD
THERE'S A LIGHT
PHANTOMS
OVER AT THE FRANKENSTEIN PLACE
JANET & BRAD
THERE'S A LIGHT
PHANTOMS
BURNING IN THE FIREPLACE
THERE'S A LIGHT—LIGHT
JANET & BRAD
IN THE DARKNESS OF EVERYBODY'S LIFE

Belinda Sinclair (Janet), London cast.

ACME
DEMOLITIO

(Lightning strikes. JANET screams.)

BRAD

It's all right, Janet.

JANET

Oh Brad let's go back. I'm cold and I'm frightened.

BRAD

Just a moment, Janet, they may have a telephone.

(BRAD pulls a cord by the curtain as though it is a bell pull. He turns to JANET, and the bell rings behind his back. After some time, the curtain opens to the far right to reveal RIFF RAFF)

RIFF RAFF

(Looking past them as if for others, or someone else.)

Hello.

BRAD

Oh: Uh: Ahh: Hi there, we're in a bit of a spot, I wonder could you help us—our car is broken down about two miles back do you have a telephone we might use . . . ?

RIFF RAFF

(Pause) You're wet.

JANET

Yes—the rain has been very heavy.

BRAD

Yes.

RIFF RAFF

Yes—*(Lightning and thunder.)*

I think you better both come inside.

JANET

You're too kind.

RIFF RAFF

(Mimics JANET.) You're too kind.

(BRAD and JANET go in, around the back of the screen to the other side of the stage. RIFF RAFF smiles and exits after them.)

(Blackout.)

Richard O'Brien (Riff Raff), London cast.

NARRATOR

(The spotlight comes up on the NARRATOR.)

And so—after braving the inclement weather, and some not too little time—it seemed that fortune had smiled on Brad and Janet and that they had found the assistance that their plight required—or had they?—There was certainly something about this house (to which, a flat tire and a wet night had brought them) that made the both of them uneasy—but, if they were to reach their destination that night, they would have to ignore such feelings and take advantage of whatever help was offered.

Following pages: Boni Enten (Columbia), Jamie Donnelly (Magenta), Bruce Scott (Riff Raff), and Tim Curry (Frank-N-Furter), Los Angeles cast.

SCENE THREE

(Interior dimly lit.)

(PHANTOMS wander set with various experimental surgical elements—i.e., brain in bottle.)

(RIFF RAFF leads BRAD and JANET onstage.. They look around. RIFF RAFF walks to the other side of the stage, stops and turns.)

RIFF RAFF

Wait here.

BRAD

(To RIFF RAFF as he exits.) Excuse me.

JANET

(Looking around.)

Oh Brad what sort of a place is this—I'm frightened.

BRAD

It's probably some sort of hunting lodge for rich weirdos—but you're shivering.

JANET

Yes, I'm wet.

BRAD

Look, feel this—there's hot air coming from this grille in the wall—take off your sweater and dry it here. I'll keep a look out for the undertaker.

JANET

(*Screams as sweater is snatched from her by hand through grill.*) Oh!

BRAD

For God's sake keep a grip on yourself Janet. I'm here—there's nothing to worry about. *(She smiles.)* Here, dry my coat too.

JANET

O.K.

(RIFF RAFF, COLUMBIA and MAGENTA enter. JANET screams.)

RIFF RAFF, COLUMBIA & MAGENTA

Master!

(A loud bang is heard from the back of the cinema as a rear door is flung open and FRANK struts onto the catwalk.)

FRANK

HOW DO YOU DO
I SEE YOU'VE MET MY FAITHFUL HANDYMAN
HE'S A LITTLE BROUGHT DOWN
BECAUSE WHEN YOU KNOCKED
HE THOUGHT YOU WERE THE CANDYMAN
DON'T GET STRUNG OUT BY THE WAY THAT
I LOOK DON'T JUDGE A BOOK BY IT'S COVER
I'M NOT MUCH OF A MAN
BY THE LIGHT OF DAY
BUT BY NIGHT I'M ONE HELL OF A LOVER

(FRANK drops his cloak. PHANTOMS, MAGENTA, COLUMBIA cheer, scream, and bow down in praise. RIFF RAFF takes the cloak and throws it into the wings.)

I'M JUST A SWEET TRANSVESTITE
FROM TRANSSEXUAL
TRANSYLVANIA.
LET ME SHOW YOU AROUND, MAYBE PLAY YOU
A SOUND YOU LOOK LIKE YOU'RE BOTH
PRETTY GROOVIE OR IF YOU WANT SOMETHING
VISUAL THAT'S NOT TOO ABYSMAL
WE COULD TAKE IN AN OLD STEVE REEVES MOVIE

BRAD

I'M GLAD WE CAUGHT YOU AT HOME
AH—COULD WE USE YOUR PHONE
WE'RE BOTH IN A BIT OF A HURRY
WE'LL JUST SAY WHERE WE ARE
THEN GO BACK TO THE CAR
WE DON'T WANT TO BE ANY WORRY

FRANK

YOU GOT CAUGHT WITH A FLAT
WELL HOW ABOUT THAT
WELL BABIES DON'T YOU PANIC

Richard O'Brien: That line, "I'm just a sweet transvestite," is powerful because it was so fucking brave and quite shocking. Women in the audience, until that exact moment, had no idea that they would find a creature like Frank that attractive. It was liberating.

BY THE LIGHT OF THE NIGHT
IT'LL ALL SEEM ALRIGHT
I'LL GET YOU A SATANIC MECHANIC
I'M JUST A
SWEET TRANSVESTITE
FROM TRANSSEXUAL
TRANSYLVANIA
WHY DON'T CHA STAY FOR THE NIGHT

RIFF RAFF, MAGENTA & COLUMBIA
NIGHT

FRANK
OR MAYBE A BITE

RIFF RAFF, MAGENTA & COLUMBIA
BITE

FRANK
I COULD SHOW YOU MY FAVOURITE OBSESSION
I'VE BEEN MAKING A MAN
WITH BLOND HAIR AND A TAN
AND HE'S GOOD FOR RELIEVING MY TENSION
I'M JUST A SWEET TRANSVESTITE
FROM TRANSSEXUAL
TRANSYLVANIA

RIFF RAFF, MAGENTA & COLUMBIA
HIT IT, HIT IT

FRANK
I'M JUST A
SWEET TRANSVESTITE
FROM TRANSSEXUAL
TRANSYLVANIA
SO COME UP TO THE LAB

(FRANK starts up the ladder leading up to the lab.)

AND SEE WHAT'S ON THE SLAB
I SEE YOU SHIVER IN ANTICI—PATION
BUT MAYBE THE RAIN
IS REALLY TO BLAME
SO I'LL REMOVE THE CAUSE
BUT NOT THE SYMPTOM

(FRANK exits behind the Laboratory curtain.)

(The SERVANTS undress JANET and BRAD. They are reduced to '50s underwear.)

BRAD

(Aside to JANET.)

It's all right, Janet, everything's gonna be all right, we'll just play along for now—and we'll pull out the aces when the time is right.

JANET

This is no time for card tricks, Brad, are you sure we'll be alright?

MAGENTA

(Snatches JANET's bag.)

No bags.

BRAD

I'm sure, Janet.

(To COLUMBIA, MAGENTA and RIFF RAFF.)

Uh. Hi there—I'm Brad Majors, this is Janet Weiss—my fiancée—
You are . . .

COLUMBIA

You're very lucky to be invited up to Frank's laboratory, a lot of people would give their right arm for the privilege.

BRAD

People like you maybe.

COLUMBIA

I've seen it.

JANET

Is he . . . is Frank . . . your husband?

RIFF RAFF

The master is not yet married, nor do I think ever will be—we are simply his servants.

Nell Campbell (Columbia), Belinda Sinclair (Janet), James Warwick (Brad), and Angela Bruce (Magenta), London cast.

JANET

Then he's very lucky.

MAGENTA

Yeah—you're lucky—I'm lucky—he's lucky—we're all lucky ...

COLUMBIA

All except Eddie.

RIFF RAFF

Sshhh!!!

(RIFF RAFF crosses to COLUMBIA with his arm raised.)

JANET

Eddie?

MAGENTA

The delivery boy.

RIFF RAFF

Sshhh!!!

(RIFF RAFF shakes his fist.)

COLUMBIA

His delivery wasn't good enough.

RIFF RAFF

(Crosses back to BRAD.)

The master only wanted to help the boy better his position.

BRAD

That's very commendable.

(BRAD slaps RIFF RAFF on the back, sending dust flying. RIFF RAFF hides his black anger.)

RIFF RAFF

Yes, it seems like only yesterday since he went ...

JANET

Where?

RIFF RAFF

To pieces.

RIFF RAFF

IT'S ASTOUNDING—TIME IS FLEETING
MADNESS
TAKES IT'S TOLL
BUT LISTEN CLOSELY—

MAGENTA & COLUMBIA

NOT FOR VERY MUCH LONGER

RIFF RAFF

I'VE GOT TO KEEP CONTROL
I REMEMBER DOING THE TIME WARP
DRINKING THOSE MOMENTS WHEN
THE BLACKNESS WOULD HIT ME—
AND THE VOID WOULD BE CALLING

ALL

LET'S DO THE TIME WARP AGAIN
LET'S DO THE TIME WARP AGAIN
(CHORUS)

NARRATOR

IT'S JUST A JUMP TO THE LEFT

ALL

AND THEN A STEP TO THE RIGHT

NARRATOR

WITH YOUR HANDS ON YOUR HIPS

ALL

YOU BRING YOUR KNEES IN TIGHT
BUT IT'S THE PELVIC THRUST
THAT STARTS TO DRIVE YOU INSANE
LET'S DO THE TIME WARP AGAIN
LET'S DO THE TIME WARP AGAIN

3,4,5. 3,4,5.
1
L R L R R
START
2

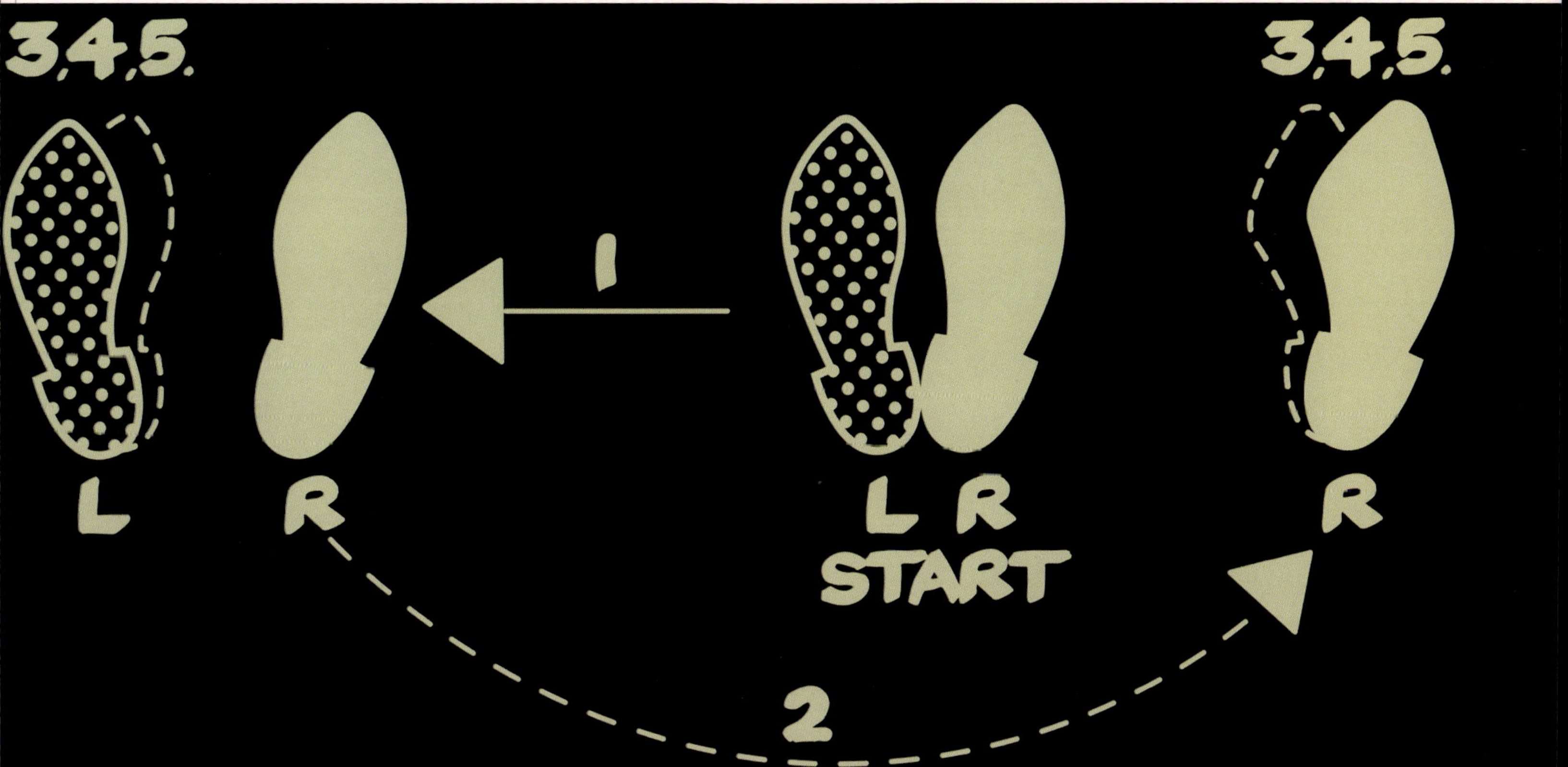

Richard O'Brien: "The Time Warp" came about during rehearsal. It was inspired by an *Astounding Tales* cover I had on my table. I looked at it and thought, "It's astounding." That's when the lyrics came together.

(COLUMBIA breaks into dance while MAGENTA and RIFF RAFF SING.)

MAGENTA

IT'S SO DREAMY—OH FANTASY FREE ME
SO YOU CAN'T SEE ME—NO NOT AT ALL
IN ANOTHER DIMENSION—WITH VOYEURISTIC
INTENTION WELL SECLUDED—I'LL SEE ALL
WITH A BIT OF A MIND FLIP—YOU'RE
THERE IN THE TIME SLIP
NOTHING CAN EVER BE THE SAME
YOU'RE SPACED OUT ON SENSATION

RIFF RAFF & MAGENTA

LIKE YOU'RE UNDER SEDATION

(RIFF RAFF drags COLUMBIA back to her place for The chorus.)

ALL

LET'S DO THE TIME WARP AGAIN
LET'S DO THE TIME WARP AGAIN

(CHORUS)

NARRATOR

IT'S JUST A JUMP TO THE LEFT

ALL

AND THEN A STEP TO THE RIGHT

NARRATOR

WITH YOUR HANDS ON YOUR HIPS

ALL

YOU BRING YOUR KNEES IN TIGHT
BUT IT'S THE PELVIC THRUST
THAT STARTS TO DRIVE YOU INSANE
LET'S DO THE TIME WARP AGAIN
LET'S DO THE TIME WARP AGAIN

COLUMBIA

WELL I WAS WALKING DOWN THE STREET
JUST HAVING A THINK
WHEN A SNAKE OF A GUY GAVE ME AN
EVIL WINK
WELL IT SHOOK ME UP, IT TOOK ME
BY SURPRISE
HE HAD A PICK UP TRUCK AND THE
DEVIL'S EYES
OH—HE STARED AT ME AND I FELT A CHANGE
TIME MEANT NOTHING—NEVER WOULD AGAIN

ALL

LET'S DO THE TIME WARP AGAIN
LET'S DO THE TIME WARP AGAIN

(COLUMBIA—Tap break.)

LET'S DO THE TIME WARP AGAIN
LET'S DO THE TIME WARP AGAIN

(CHORUS)

NARRATOR

IT'S JUST A JUMP TO THE LEFT

ALL

AND THEN A STEP TO THE RIGHT

NARRATOR

WITH YOUR HANDS ON YOUR HIPS

ALL

YOU BRING YOUR KNEES IN TIGHT
BUT IT'S THE PELVIC THRUST
THAT STARTS TO DRIVE YOU INSANE
LET'S DO THE TIME WARP AGAIN
LET'S DO THE TIME WARP AGAIN

(Blackout.)

(COLUMBIA, RIFF RAFF, and MAGENTA exit, leaving BRAD and JANET alone

Jim Sharman: If we're talking about the beginning of a cult, it started with "Time Warp." Richard also did the original choreography, which I suspect he and Kimi had refined, but the idea itself never changed from the start.

Nell Campbell (Columbia), Richard O'Brien (Riff Raff), Patricia Quinn (Magenta), and Jonathan Adams (Narrator), London cast.

SCENE FOUR

(The lights come up and FRANK appears, dressed in a green surgical gown as he pulls on surgical rubber gloves.)

FRANK

Unlock a mind—unmind a lock—its the same as the beginning of the end—do you follow?

JANET

No.

BRAD

It's an anagram, Janet.

FRANK

(Wincing at BRAD's stupidity.)

I wonder may I offer you something refreshing?

BRAD & JANET

No.

FRANK

No. You're right, I won't—how delightful to have fresh faces around. Magenta—Columbia—go and assist Riff Raff—I will entertain Ahh.

BRAD

Brad Majors.

FRANK

(FRANK shakes BRAD's hand.)

Brad Majors.

BRAD

And this is my fiancée Janet Weiss.

(He pronounces it "Vice.")

JANET

Weiss.

BRAD

Weiss.

FRANK

Enchanted. How nice—and what charming under-clothes you both have—but here, put these on.

(He hands JANET a lab coat and helps BRAD on with his, during speech.)

They'll make you feel less vulnerable.
We don't often receive visitors here, let alone
show them hospitality . . .

BRAD

Hospitality! All we wanted was to use your phone, a
reasonable request which you have
chosen to ignore.

JANET

Don't be ungrateful, Brad.

BRAD

Ungrateful!

FRANK

How forceful you are, Brad, what a perfect example
of manhood—so dominant—you must be
very proud, Janet.

JANET

Yes.

FRANK

Tell me Brad, do you have any tattoos?

BRAD

Certainly not.

FRANK

Oh well . . .

(To JANET.)

How about you?

(RIFF RAFF pokes his head around the curtain in the laboratory. He is wearing a green surgical cap and gown.)

RIFF RAFF

Everything is in readiness, Master.
We merely wait for you to give the word.

(MAGENTA and COLUMBIA enter.)

FRANK

Tonight Brad and Janet, you are to witness
a new breakthrough in Biochemical
research and paradise is to be mine . . .

JANET

Oh how wonderful for you.

FRANK

Yes. It was strange the way it happened . . . one of those quirks of fate really . . . one of those moments when . . . everything looks black, the chips are down, your back is against the wall. You panic—you're trapped—there's no way out and even if there was it would probably be a one way ticket to the bottom of the bay. And then suddenly you get a break—all the pieces seem to fit into place—what a sucker you'd been—what a fool—the answer was there all the time—it took a small accident to make it happen.

(All look at FRANK in amazement.)

An accident.

MAGENTA & COLUMBIA

An accident.

FRANK

That's how I discovered the secret—
that elusive ingredient—that
spark that is the breath of life.
Yes.
I have that knowledge,
I hold the key to life itself,
you see.
Brad and Janet, you are fortunate. for
tonight is the night my beautiful
creature is destined to be born.

Jamie Donnelly (Magenta), Boni Enten (Columbia), Tim Curry (Frank-N-Furter), Abigale Haness (Janet), and Bill Miller (Brad), Los Angeles cast.

FRANK

(To RIFF RAFF.)

Throw open the switches on the Sonic Oscillator
and step up the Reactor
Power Input . . . three more points.

(FRANK climbs to the laboratory. RIFF RAFF pulls back the curtains to reveal ROCKY lying like a mummy on the Coca-Cola fridge. Lights flash and the band plays an uneasy chord that throughout this exchange.)

(3 CHORDS—1, 2, 3.)

JANET

Brad!

BRAD

It's alright Janet.

FRANK

Balls

(3 Chords.)

JANET

Brad!

BRAD

It's alright Janet.

FRANK

Tubes

(3 Chords.)

JANET

Brad!

BRAD

It's alright Janet.

FRANK

Crimps

(3 Chords.)
(ROCKY is revealed in swaddling clothes.)
(FRANK disrobes him during the song.)

Richard O'Brien (Riff Raff), Rayner Bourton (Rocky), and Tim Curry (Frank-N-Furter), London cast.

THE SWORD OF DAMOCLES

ROCKY
THE SWORD OF DAMOCLES IS HANGING OVER MY HEAD
AND I'VE GOT THE FEELING SOMEONE IS GONNA BE
CUTTING THE THREAD
(FRANK is thrilled; ROCKY is terrified.)
OH WHO IS ME—MY LIFE IS A MISERY
OH CAN'T YOU SEE I'M AT THE START
OF A PRETTY BIG DOWNER
(ROCKY dances away from FRANK, who chases him throughout the song.)
I WOKE UP THIS MORNING WITH A START WHEN
I FELL OUT OF THE BED
ALL
THAT AIN'T NO CRIME
ROCKY
AND LEFT FROM MY DREAMING WAS A FEELING
OF UNAMIABLE DREAD
ALL
THAT AIN'T NO CRIME
ROCKY
MY HIGH IS LOW—I'M DRESSED UP WITH NO PLACE
TO GO AND ALL I KNOW IS I'M AT THE
START OF A PRETTY BIG DOWNER
ALL
(SHA LA LA LA THAT AIN'T NO CRIME)
(SHA LA LA LA THAT AIN'T NO CRIME)
(SHA LA LA LA THAT AIN'T NO CRIME)
(THAT AIN'T NO CRIME)
NARRATOR
(Spoken)
ROCKY HORROR YOU NEED PEACE OF MIND—AND I

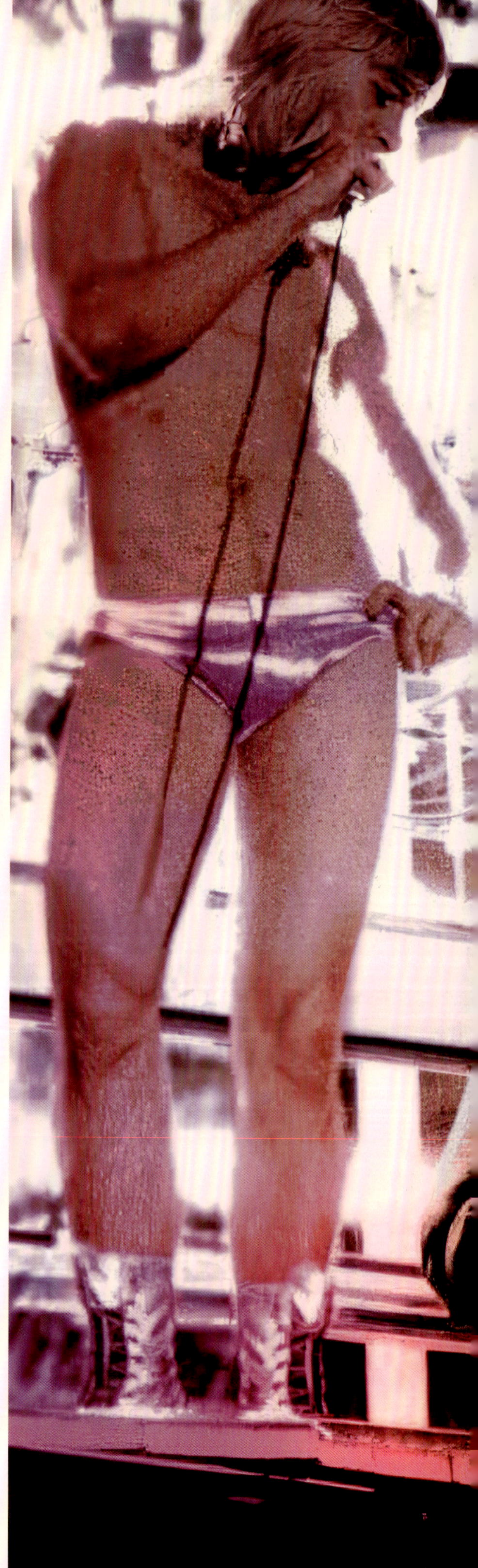

WANT TO TELL YOU THAT YOU'RE DOING
JUST FINE
YOU'RE THE PRODUCT OF ANOTHER TIME AND
FEELING DOWN WELL THAT'S NO CRIME

ALL

THAT AIN'T NO CRIME

ROCKY

THE SWORD OF DAMOCLES IS HANGING
OVER MY HEAD

ALL

THAT AIN'T NO CRIME

ROCKY

AND I'VE GOT THE FEELING THAT
SOMEONE'S GOING TO BE CUTTING THE THREAD

ALL

THAT AIN'T NO CRIME

ROCKY

OH WOE IS ME—MY LIFE IS A MYSTERY
OH CAN'T YOU SEE THAT I'M AT THE START
OF A PRETTY BIG DOWNER

ALL

SHA LA LA LA THAT AIN'T NO CRIME
SHA LA LA LA THAT AIN'T NO CRIME
SHA LA LA LA THAT AIN'T NO CRIME
THAT AIN'T NO CRIME
SHA LA LA LA THAT AIN'T NO CRIME
SHA LA LA LA THAT AIN'T NO CRIME
(SHA LA LA LA THAT AIN'T NO CRIME)
THAT AIN'T NO CRIME
SHA LA LA

(ROCKY jumps on the box and shows his biceps.)

Rayner Bourton (Rocky) and Tim Curry (Frank-N-Furter), London cast.

FRANK

Well really—that's no way to behave on your first day out.

(The NARRATOR holds up a mirror to ROCKY.)

ROCKY

Well nobody's perfect—But I do think you made a pretty good job of the body work.

FRANK

You are the result of many hours of toil—and now my beautiful creature you're ready for the ultimate test.

ROCKY

Oh dear.

FRANK

But first meet the family. Well, Riff Raff, what do you think?

RIFF RAFF

He's a credit to my/your genius.

FRANK

Magenta?

Tim Curry (Frank-N-Furter), Rayner Bourton (Rocky), Belinda Sinclair (Janet), and Chris Malcolm (Brad), London cast.

FRANK

A WEAKLING WEIGHING 98 POUNDS
GETS SAND IN HIS FACE WHEN KICKED
TO THE GROUND
AND SOON IN THE GYM
WITH A DETERMINED CHIN
THE SWEAT FROM HIS PORES
AS HE WORKS FOR HIS CAUSE
WILL MAKE HIM GLISTEN AND GLEAM
AND WITH MASSAGE AND JUST A BIT OF STEAM
HE'LL BE PINK BUT QUITE CLEAN
HE'LL BE A STRONG MAN

ALL

BUT THE WRONG MAN

FRANK

HE'LL EAT NUTRITIOUS HIGH-PROTEIN
AND SWALLOW RAW EGGS
(ROCKY does whatever gymnastics he can.)
TRY TO BUILD UP HIS SHOULDERS
CHEST, ARMS AND LEGS
SUCH AN EFFORT
IF ONLY HE KNEW OF MY PLAN
WHEN IN JUST SEVEN DAYS
I CAN MAKE YOU A MAN
HE'LL DO PRESS UPS AND CHIN UPS
THE SNATCH CLEAN AND JERK
DYNAMIC TENSION
MUST BE AWFULLY HARD WORK
SUCH STRENUOUS LIVING
I JUST DON'T UNDERSTAND
WHEN IN JUST SEVEN DAYS
I CAN MAKE YOU A MAN

London cast.

DRINK

(A drum roll, the spotlight reveals the Coca Cola cooler. COLUMBIA rushes to open it.)

COLUMBIA

Eddie!

(The cast freezes in an animated tableau. EDDIE appears from the cooler beaten and battered. His part rockabilly bad boy and part Frankenstein's monster. He grabs a microphone from COLUMBIA, who clearly adores him.)

Meat Loaf (Eddie), Los Angeles cast.

HOT PATOOTIE (BLESS MY SOUL)

EDDIE

WHATEVER HAPPENED TO SATURDAY NIGHT
WHEN YOU DRESSED UP SHARP AND YOU FELT ALRIGHT
IT DON'T SEEM THE SAME SINCE COSMIC LIGHT
CAME INTO MY LIFE AND I THOUGHT I WAS DIVINE
I USED TO GO FOR A RIDE WITH A CHICK WHO'D GO
AND LISTEN TO THE MUSIC ON THE RADIO
A SAXOPHONE WAS BLOWING ON A ROCK AND ROLL SHOW
AND YOU CLIMBED IN THE BACK AND YOU REALLY
HAD
A GOOD TIME

(The tableau comes alive and they all dance.)

ALL

HOT PATOOTIE BLESS MY SOUL
I REALLY LOVE THAT ROCK AND ROLL
HOT PATOOTIE BLESS MY SOUL
I REALLY LOVE THAT ROCK AND ROLL
HOT PATOOTIE BLESS MY SOUL
I REALLY LOVE THAT ROCK AND ROLL
HOT PATOOTIE BLESS MY SOUL
I REALLY LOVE THAT ROCK AND ROLL

(ALL freeze again.)

EDDIE

MY HEAD USED TO SWIM FROM THE PERFUME I SMELT
MY HANDS KIND OF FUMBLED WITH HER WHITE PLASTIC
BELT
I'D TASTE HER BABY PINK LIPSTICK AND THAT'S
WHEN I'D MELT

Paddy O'Hagan (Eddie), London cast.

DRINK

AND SHE'D WHISPER IN MY EAR TONIGHT SHE REALLY
WAS MINE
GET BACK IN FRONT AND PUT SOME HAIR OIL ON
BUDDY HOLLY WAS SINGING HIS VERY LAST SONG
WITH YOUR ARM ROUND YOUR GIRL YOU'D TRY TO
SING ALONG
YOU FELT PRETTY GOOD 'CAUSE YOU'D REALLY HAD
A GOOD TIME

(Everyone comes alive again. FRANK takes off his surgical gown.)

ALL

HOT PATOOTIE BLESS MY SOUL
I REALLY LOVE THAT ROCK AND ROLL
HOT PATOOTIE BLESS MY SOUL
I REALLY LOVE THAT ROCK AND ROLL
HOT PATOOTIE BLESS MY SOUL
I REALLY LOVE THAT ROCK AND ROLL
HOT PATOOTIE BLESS MY SOUL
I REALLY LOVE THAT ROCK AND ROLL
HOT PATOOTIE BLESS MY SOUL
I REALLY LOVE THAT ROCK AND ROLL
HOT PATOOTIE BLESS MY SOUL
I REALLY LOVE THAT ROCK AND ROLL
HOT PATOOTIE BLESS MY SOUL
I REALLY LOVE THAT ROCK AND ROLL
HOT PATOOTIE BLESS MY SOUL
I REALLY LOVE THAT ROCK AND ROLL

Richard Hartley: Meat Loaf completely rephrased "Hot Patootie," especially the verses. Richard had nothing to do with that; we just gave Meat Loaf space to work.

Meat Loaf (Eddie), Los Angeles cast.

(FRANK chases EDDIE back to the cooler and stabs him to death with the microphone stand. He stuffs EDDIE back into the cooler, slams the lid shut, and sits on it.)

(COLUMBIA is distraught.)

FRANK

One from the vaults.

(He transforms her mood.)

Columbia

ROCKY

How can you keep him around?
He's so ugly.

FRANK

A certain naïve charm.
But no muscle.
We had a mental relationship—

Tim Curry (Frank-N-Furter) and Nell Campbell (Columbia), London cast.

FRANK

BUT A DELTOID AND A BICEP
A HOT GROIN AND A TRICEP
MAKES ME SHAKE
MAKES ME WANT TO TAKE
CHARLES ATLAS BY THE HAND

PHANTOMS

IN JUST SEVEN DAYS I CAN MAKE YOU A MAN

FRANK

I DON'T WANT NO DISSENSION
JUST DYNAMIC TENSION

JANET

I'M A MUSCLE FAN

(She throws herself at ROCKY.)

ALL

IN JUST SEVEN DAYS I CAN MAKE YOU A MAN

FRANK

DIG IN IF YOU CAN

(He throws JANET back at BRAD.)

ALL

IN JUST SEVEN DAYS I CAN MAKE YOU A MAN

(Band plays "WEDDING MARCH.")
(MAGENTA and COLUMBIA give FRANK a bouquet and veil.)
(PHANTOMS throw confetti.)
(Wedding procession takes place.)
(FRANK throws the bouquet.)
(RIFF RAFF catches it.)
(Everyone exits except the NARRATOR.)
(Curtain)

END OF ACT I

London cast.

ROCKY
HORROR
SHOW

ACT II

ENTR'ACT

(NARRATOR enters on last bar of "Time Warp.")

NARRATOR

There are those who say life is an illusion—
And reality as we know it, is merely a
figment of our imaginations.
If this is so, Brad and Janet are quite safe.
But—there are some who have a far more physical philosophy—
those who would stop at nothing to satisfy their base
desires—It could be that Brad and Janet are among those
who hold the devil's reins.

(Blackout)

SCENE FIVE

"JANET'S ROOM"

(Voices in Blackout.)

(Action in both scenes should he exactly the same.)

JANET

Oh Brad—Oh Yes—Yes my darling—What if—

(A single light comes up revealing, in silhouette, a man lying on top of a woman.)

BRAD

It's all right Janet—everything's going to be all right.

JANET

Oh I hope so my darling. I'm so fri . . .

(All Lights come on and the man's short-haired wig comes off.)

You!

(The man comes up on his knees, revealing himself to be FRANK, not BRAD.)

FRANK

I'm afraid so, Janet. But wasn't it nice . . .

JANET

You beast—you monster—what have you done with Brad?

FRANK

Mmm—nothing—why, do you think I should?

JANET

You tricked me—I wouldn't have—I've never—Oh my God—never.

(FRANK removes condom and throws it away.)

FRANK

I know—but it wasn't all bad, was it?
Not really even half bad—in fact, I think perhaps you found it quite—pleasurable—Mmm—so soft so—sensual.

JANET

Ahh—no—stop—I mean help—
I—Brad—Ohhh—Brad.

FRANK

Shh. Brad's probably asleep by now—do you want him to see you like this?

JANET

Like this? Like how?

FRANK

Like this.

JANET

It's your fault, you're to blame . . .
I was—saving myself.

FRANK

Well I'm sure you're not spent yet
and it was an enjoyable
experience was it not?

(Lights dim.)

You did like it, didn't you? There's no crime in giving yourself over to pleasure—is there? We could try for an action replay—Oh Janet you've wasted so much time already—Brad needn't know. I won't tell him, Mmmm.

(Blackout)

JANET

Are you sure you won't tell him? Ohhh . . .

SCENE SIX

"BRAD'S ROOM"

(Voices in blackout.)

JANET

Oh Brad—Oh yes—Yes my darling, but what if . . .

(A Light comes up revealing, in silhouette, a man lying on top of a "woman.")

BRAD

It's all right Janet—everything's going to be all right.

JANET

I hope so my darling.

(The Lights come up, and the long wig comes off, revealing it to be FRANK.)

BRAD

You!

FRANK

I'm afraid so Brad—but wasn't it nice . . .

BRAD

You fiend, you scoundrel—what have you done with Janet?

FRANK

Mmm—nothing—why, do you think I should?

BRAD

You tricked me, I wouldn't have—I've never—
Oh my God—never.

(FRANK removes condom from BRAD.)

FRANK

I know—but it wasn't all bad was it?
Not really even half bad, in fact, I think you found it quite pleasurable—Oh so soft—so sensual.

BRAD

Ah—Help—No—stop. I mean—
Janet—Ohh—Janet.

FRANK

Shh—Janet's probably asleep by now—Do you want her to see you like this?

Chris Malcolm (Brad) and Tim Curry (Frank-N-Furter), London cast.

BRAD

Like this like how—

FRANK

Like this.

BRAD

It's your fault. You're to blame—I thought it was the real thing.

FRANK

Oh come on Brad admit it. It was enjoyable wasn't it? You liked it didn't you? There's no crime in giving yourself over to pleasure—is there?

(Lights dim.)

We could try for an action replay. Oh Brad you've wasted so much time already—Janet needn't know. I won't tell her—Mmm . . .

(Blackout)

BRAD

Are you sure you won't tell her—Ohhh . . .

RIFF RAFF

(Over the intercom.)

Master—the laboratory is empty. Rocky has vanished—the new playmate is loose and somewhere in the building.

FRANK

Oh—Wow—What a—Mmm—Oh—Coming.

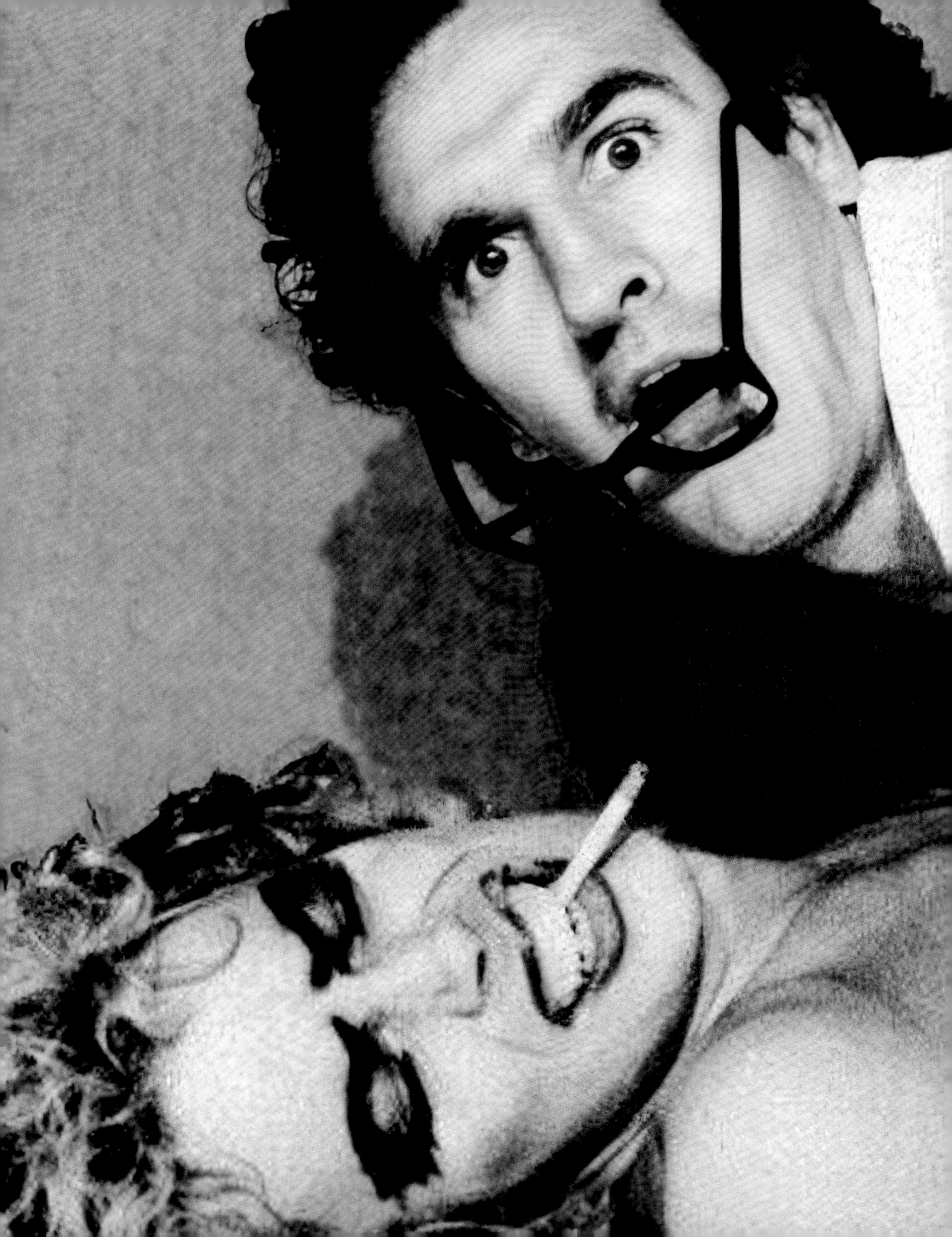

SCENE SEVEN

LABORATORY

(Enter JANET.)

JANET

What's happening here—Where's Brad?—Where's anybody? If only we hadn't made this journey—if only the car hadn't broken down—if only we were amongst friends or sane persons.

(The NARRATOR enters.)

NARRATOR

If and only—two small words that kept repeating themselves again and again in Janet's thoughts, but it was too late to go back now—it was as if she were riding a giant tidal wave, it would be folly to fight against it—her only chance would be to ride it out—adapt—and perhaps also—survive.

(JANET wanders toward the laboratory. The curtain is pulled back by ROCKY. They both jump.)

ROCKY

Oh! Its you—look I'm trying to hide from my creator and his minion—they scare me—I feel that all is not well here. I have been thinking a lot about—*(Eddie)* I have a feeling of foreboding.

JANET

It's all like some terrible dream.

ROCKY

Is it true you don't like men with too many muscles?

JANET

Well . . .

ROCKY

Have you got any lip gloss?

JANET

I'm engaged to Brad, just the same as Betty Munroe was to Ralf Hapshatt. But Frank's kisses overwhelmed me with an ecstasy I had never dreamed of before—hot burning kisses—I could see Brad's face before me, and my mind screamed—No!—but my lips were hungry, too hungry—I wanted to be loved, and loved completely——Oh Brad, Brad my darling how could I have done this to you.

ROCKY

This room is a womb to me.

JANET

Yes—there you see, it's instinctive—you returned here for one thing—security. Oh where's Brad—?

(JANET fiddles with the TV monitor. The TV monitor can be a pretend remote switch which seems to throw slides on the gauze screen. Or it can be an old TV set under a ladder or hung over the Audience so that they can see it, but not its screen.)

What have they done with him?

NARRATOR

Janet's feelings ran wild as she frantically manipulated the selector switch on the TV monitor—The screen threw up images of empty rooms and corridors—finally she stopped—at Frank's bedroom.

(Janet sees FRANK kissing BRAD.)

JANET

Aaahhh!

NARRATOR

Aaahhh!

ROCKY

Oh, you can't rely on anyone.

JANET

Oh Brad!—How could you?

(They all bend over trying to work out the position on screen.)

NARRATOR

If one is suffering from the pangs of remorse for a sexual indiscretion—it would seem logical that the transgressor would be sympathetic toward a loved one caught committing a similar misdemeanor—But emotion is an irrational and powerful master—and from what Janet witnessed on the monitor—there seemed little doubt that she was indeed its slave.

(COLUMBIA and MAGENTA enter with glasses of champagne and sit on the Coke machine, sipping their drinks.)

MAGENTA & COLUMBIA

Tell us about it, Janet.

TOUCH-A, TOUCH-A, TOUCH ME

JANET
I WAS FEELING DONE IN
COULDN'T WIN
I'D ONLY EVER KISSED BEFORE
MAGENTA & COLUMBIA
YOU MEAN SHE'D ONLY EVER KISSED
JANET
AHA
I THOUGHT THERE'S NO USE GETTING
INTO HEAVY PETTING
IT ONLY LEADS TO TROUBLE
AND SEAT WETTING
NOW ALL I WANT TO KNOW
IS HOW TO GO
I'VE TASTED BLOOD AND I WANT MORE.
MAGENTA & COLUMBIA
MORE, MORE, MORE
JANET
I'LL PUT UP NO RESISTANCE
I WANT TO STAY THE DISTANCE
I'VE GOT AN ITCH TO SCRATCH
AND I NEED ASSISTANCE
(CHORUS)
TOUCH-A TOUCH-A TOUCH-A-TOUCH ME
I WANT TO BE DIRTY
THRILL ME CHILL ME FULFILL ME
CREATURE OF THE NIGHT
THEN IF ANYTHING GROWS
WHEN YOU POSE
I'LL OIL YOU UP AND RUB YOU DOWN
MAGENTA & COLUMBIA
DOWN, DOWN, DOWN
AND THAT'S JUST ONE SMALL FRACTION
OF THE MAIN ATTRACTION
YOU NEED A FRIENDLY HAND
AND I NEED ACTION
(JANET and ROCKY climb to the laboratory and onto the bed.)
JANET
TOUCH-A TOUCH-A TOUCH-A-TOUCH ME
I WANT TO BE DIRTY
THRILL ME CHILL ME FULFILL ME
CREATURE OF THE NIGHT
TOUCH-A TOUCH-A TOUCH-A-TOUCH ME
I WANT TO BE DIRTY
THRILL ME CHILL ME FULFILL ME
CREATURE OF THE NIGHT
TOUCH-A TOUCH-A TOUCH-A-TOUCH ME
I WANT TO BE DIRTY
THRILL ME CHILL ME FULFILL ME
CREATURE OF THE NIGHT
CREATURE OF THE NIGHT
CREATURE OF THE NIGHT
(Blackout)

Belinda Sinclair: "Touch Me" was my favorite song to sing because I sang half of it upside down, with my legs around Rocky's waist, then fell back and finished the song right side up.

Patricia Quinn (Magenta) and Nell Campbell (Columbia), London cast.

DRINK
Coca-Cola

SCENE EIGHT

(The lights come up on stage as FRANK enters, chasing RIFF RAFF and whipping him. FRANK is wearing a leather moto jacket over his corset. BRAD follows. The NARRATOR is already on stage.)

RIFF RAFF

Aaaggghhh!—Mercy! Master

FRANK

(Whipping Riff Raff)

How did it happen? I understood
you were to be watching.

RIFF RAFF

I was only away for a moment, Master . . .

FRANK

See if you can find him on the monitor.
Oh Magenta. Oh Rocky. Oh Rocky. Oh Rocky.

(Click—BRAD's empty room—switch—switch—switch—JANET's room.)

RIFF RAFF

I've located him in the female's quarters, Master.

FRANK

Rocky! I think I'm going to . . .

(FRANK is about to faint, but sees that noone is around to catch him. FRANK composes himself, calls RIFF RAFF over, and faints into his arms. RIFF RAFF catches him just in time.)

BRAD

(Enters, sees TV.)

Janet! How could she? That's it—it's over.

NARRATOR

Over! What was over? Not the night that was certain. Brad and Janet's engagement? Their love for one another? Who could say—for questions such as these are not to be answered by the academic, they must be left for the heart to solve and Brad you may be sure, had plenty of heart.

BRAD
ONCE IN A WHILE
SHE DON'T WANT TO CALL YOU
SPEAKING ON THE TELEPHONE
AND ONCE IN YOUR LIFE
SHE DON'T WANT TO KNOW YOU
YOU LOOK AROUND
THE ONE YOU FOUND
SHE IS GONE
NARRATOR
HUMMINAH HUMMINAH HUMMINAH HUMMINAH HUM
(PHANTOMS appear as back-up singers dressed as JANET.)
BRAD
AND THAT'S ALL THE TIME
THAT IT TAKES
FOR A HEART TO TURN TO STONE
THE SWEETER THE WINE
THE HARDER TO MAKE THE BREAK
YOU HEAR SOMETHING
ABOUT SOMEONE YOU THOUGHT YOU'D KNOWN
SO BABY DON'T CRY
LIKE THERE'S NO TOMORROW
AFTER THE NIGHT THERE'S BRAND NEW DAY
AND THERE'LL BE NO PAIN
AND NO MORE SORROW
SO WASH YOUR FACE
AND PHONE MY PLACE. IT'LL BE OKAY
AND THAT'S ALL THE TIME
THAT IT TAKES
FOR A HEART TO BEAT AGAIN
SO GIVE ME A SIGN
THAT A LOVER MAKES
YOU LOOK AROUND THE ONE
FOUND IS BACK AGAIN . . . IS BACK AGAIN
PHANTOMS
IS BACK AGAIN
BRAD & PHANTOMS
IS BACK AGAIN
IS BACK AGAIN
IS BACK AGAIN
IS BACK AGAIN
BRAD
IS BACK AGAIN

Christopher Malcolm (Brad), London cast.

(FRANK and RIFF RAFF enter.)

FRANK

How maudlin—how pathetic—Your baggage has
dared to defile my beautiful creature—
Oh Rocky how could you?

RIFF RAFF

(Static is heard from the monitor. Someone outside is creeping up on the hidden camera.)

Master—we have a visitor.

FRANK

Oh shit.

BRAD

Great Scott—Scotty—
Dr. Evrett Scott.

RIFF RAFF

You know this earth—

(FRANK stops RIFF RAFF.)

FRANK

This person.

BRAD

Yes, I do. He's an old friend of mine.

FRANK

I see—so this wasn't simply a chance meeting—
you came here with a purpose.

BRAD

That's not true—my car broke down—I told you.

FRANK

I know what you told me, Brad—but this Dr. Evrett Scott, his name is not unknown to me.

BRAD

He was a science teacher at Denton High.

FRANK

And now he works for your Government—doesn't he, Brad? He's attached to the bureau of the investigation of that which you call UFO's—that's right, isn't it, Brad?

BRAD

He might be—I don't know.

(*A figure in a wheelchair crosses the audience from right to left. No one on stage sees him.*)

RIFF RAFF

The intruder is entering the building, Master.

FRANK

Ah he's in the Zen room.
Seal off all exits—and all doors—except for those that lead here—Riff Raff—bring Rocky and Janet here—I think we should make this a social occasion. The three unexpected guests shall entertain us with a floor show—which I shall direct.

(FRANK makes a signal and door opens revealing DR. SCOTT.)

SCENE NINE

(DR. SCOTT, in a wheelchair pushed by COLUMBIA, enters left. RIFF RAFF enters the laboratory and MAGENTA comes on stage.)

COLUMBIA

Hi—Ho—Silver.

BRAD

Dr. Scott!

SCOTTY

Brad—what are you doing here?

FRANK

Don't play games, Dr. Scott. It was part of your plan, was it not, that Brad Majors and his female should check the layout for you—unfortunately for you all there is to be a change of plans—I'm sure you're adaptable, Dr. Scott—I know Brad is.

SCOTTY

I can assure you that Brad's presence here comes as a complete surprise to me. As does the set up you have here— I didn't expect it to be quite so . . .

(He goes to inspect laboratory.)

FRANK

Sophisticated—Dr. Scott? Or should I say Dr. Von Scott?

BRAD

What exactly are you implying?

SCOTTY

They didn't prove nothink! Ah—this machine here . . .

(He examines the cooler and takes a picture of it.)

BRAD

What do you think it is, Doc?

SCOTTY

At this precise moment it's hard to tell—but it seems to be made of a metal that is not of this earth— I would say it was from another planet.

Tim Curry (Frank-N-Furter) and Paddy O'Hagan (Dr. Scott), London cast.

(JANET and ROCKY are revealed in lab.)
(The following dialogue should be repeated exactly the same each time.)

JANET

Brad!

SCOTTY

Janet!

FRANK

Rocky!

JANET

Dr. Scott! Brad!

SCOTTY

Janet!

FRANK

Rocky!

JANET

Dr. Scott! Brad!

SCOTTY

Janet!

FRANK

Rocky!

JANET

Dr. Scott!

FRANK

Oh Rocky.Oh Rocky!

ROCKY

Piss off.

FRANK

Listen—I made him and I can break him just as easily—I'll pull his plug out.

SCOTTY

I suppose you intend to do with us
as you did for Eddie.

PHANTOMS

Sshh!

COLUMBIA

Eddie!

MAGENTA & RIFF RAFF

Sshh!

BRAD

Eddie—I've seen him, he looks terrible.

PHANTOMS

Sshh!

FRANK

What do you know of Eddie, Dr. Scott?

SCOTTY

I happen to know a great deal about a lot of things—
you see Eddie
happens to be my nephew.

BRAD

Dr. Scott!

SCOTTY

Yes, Brad—my sister's boy. I knew he was in
with a bad crowd, but it was worse than
I imagined—aliens.

BRAD

Tell them, Doc.

*(Everyone gathers around DR. SCOTT.
BRAD hands him the microphone.)*

EDDIE'S TEDDY

SCOTTY
FROM THE DAY HE WAS BORN HE WAS TROUBLE
HE WAS THE THORN
IN HIS MOTHER'S SIDE
SHE TRIED IN VAIN
NARRATOR
BUT HE NEVER CAUSED HER NOTHING BUT PAIN
SCOTTY
HE LEFT HOME THE DAY SHE DIED EIN
SWEI TREI
FROM THE DAY SHE WAS GONE
ALL HE WANTED
WAS A ROCKIN' ROLL PORN AND A MOTOR BIKE
SHOOTIN' UP JUNK
NARRATOR
HE WAS A LOW DOWN CHEAP LITTLE PUNK
SCOTTY
TAKING EVERYONE FOR A RIDE
ALL
WHEN EDDIE SAID HE DIDN'T LIKE HIS TEDDY
YOU KNEW HE WAS A NO GOOD KID
BUT WHEN HE THREATENED YOUR LIFE
WITH A SWITCH BLADE KNIFE
FRANK
WHAT A GUY
COLUMBIA
MADE YOU CRY
SCOTTY
AND I DID
(COLUMBIA starts climbing a ladder)
COLUMBIA
EVERYBODY SHOVED HIM
I VERY NEARLY LOVED HIM
I SAY HEY LISTEN TO ME
STAY SANE INSIDE INSANITY
BUT HE LOCKED THE DOOR AND THREW
AWAY THE KEY
SCOTTY
BUT HE MUST HAVE BEEN DRAWN
INTO SOMETHING
MAKING HIM WARN ME IN A
NOTE WHICH READ
(*SCOTTY pulls out a*
blood-stained note.)
ALL
WHAT'S IT SAY, WHAT'S IT SAY?
SCOTTY
I'M OUT OF MY HEAD
NARRATOR
HURRY OR I MAY BE DEAD
SCOTTY
THEY MUSTN'T CARRY OUT THEIR
EVIL DEEDS
ALL
WHEN EDDIE SAID HE DIDN'T LIKE
HIS TEDDY
YOU KNEW HE WAS A NO GOOD KID
BUT WHEN HE THREATENED YOUR LIFE
WITH A SWITCH BLADE KNIFE
WHEN EDDIE SAID HE DIDN'T LIKE
HIS TEDDY
YOU KNEW HE WAS A NO GOOD KID
BUT WHEN HE THREATENED YOUR LIFE
WITH A SWITCH BLADE KNIFE

London cast.

FRANK
WHAT A GUY
SCOTTY
MAKES YOU CRY
COLUMBIA
AND I DID
ALL
HEY HEY HEY
FRANK
WHAT A GUY
SCOTTY
MAKES YOU CRY
COLUMBIA
AND I DID
ALL
HEY HEY HEY
FRANK
WHAT A GUY
SCOTTY
MAKES YOU CRY
COLUMBIA
AND I DID
ALL
YEAH YEAH YEAH
FRANK
WHAT A GUY
COLUMBIA
MAKES YOU CRY
SCOTTY
AND SHE DID
ALL
YES SHE DID
SCOTTY & COLUMBIA
AND WE DID
ALL
YES WE DID
EDDIE

Tim Curry (Frank-N-Furter), Meat Loaf (Dr. Scott), Graham Jarvis (Narrator), Jamie Donnelly (Magenta), Abigail Haness (Janet), Kim Milford (Rocky), and Bill Miller (Brad), Los Angeles cast.

(FRANK runs to the Coke cooler.)

FRANK

Say a prayer for Eddie, I just defrosted him.

(He pulls out a bag of blood and gore.)

His destiny is in the bag.

BRAD

Why you . . .

FRANK

(Flicks a switch.)

(Three pools of light fall on the stage, one each on BRAD, JANET, and SCOTTY.)

There, that should restrain you all. Magenta.

(He holds out the bag.)

MAGENTA

I'll put him down the waste disposal.

FRANK

Clever girl.

(FRANK throws the bag to MAGENTA. MAGENTA exits with the bag.)

JANET

My feet—there's something wrong with my feet.

SCOTTY

My wheels! My God! I can't move my wheels.

BRAD

It's as if we're glued to the spot.

FRANK

You are, so quake with fear you tiny fools—O.K. it's startime—Riff Raff set the sonic transducer on program 8 secure all levels at zero—

MAGENTA

Relax.

SCOTTY

You won't find earth people quite the easy mark that you imagine—this sonic transducer! It is I suppose some type of audio vibratory physiomolecular transport device!

FRANK

You'd better believe it, baby.

BRAD

You mean . . . ?

SCOTTY

Yes, Brad—it's something we ourselves have been working on. But it seems our friend here has found a way of perfecting it and then projecting it through space and who knows, perhaps even time itself.

JANET

You mean he's going to send us to another planet?

WISE UP JANET WEISS

FRANK
PLANET-SHMANET JANET
TELL YOU ONCE
WON'T TELL YOU TWICE
YOU'D BETTER WISE UP JANET WEISS
Y'APPLE PIE
DON'T TASTE TOO NICE
YOU'D BETTER WISE UP JANET WEISS
I'VE LAID THE SEED
IT SHOULD BE ALL YOU NEED
YOU'RE AS SENSUAL
AS A PENCIL
WOUND UP LIKE AN 'E' OR FIRST STRING
WHEN WE MADE IT
DID JA HEAR A BELL RING?
Y'GOT A BLOCK
TAKE MY ADVICE
YOU'D BETTER WISE UP JANET WEISS
THE TRANSDUCER
WILL SEDUCE YAH
IT'S SOMETHING YOU'LL GET USED TO
A MENTAL MIND-FUCK CAN BE NICE
YOU'D BETTER WISE UP—JANET WEISS
YOU'D BETTER WISE UP
BUILD YOUR THIGHS UP
YOU'D BETTER WISE UP
NARRATOR
AND THEN SHE CRIES OUT
JANET
STOP!
(RIFF RAFF comes down from the laboratory, picks up a spray gun, and dances to the stage.)
FRANK
DON'T GET HOT AND FLUSTERED
USE A BIT OF MUSTARD
(FRANK signals MAGENTA who pulls switch and releases them as RIFF RAFF sprays them. COLUMBIA takes them off stage.)
ALL
YOU'RE A HOT DOG
BUT YOU'D BETTER NOT TRY TO HURT HER
FRANK FURTER
(BRAD is taken off by COLUMBIA.)
YOU'RE A HOT DOG
BUT YOU'D BETTER NOT TRY TO HURT HER
FRANK FURTER
(SCOTTY is taken off.)
YOU'RE A HOT DOG
BUT YOU'D BETTER NOT TRY TO HURT HER
FRANK FURTER
(JANET and ROCKY are taken off.)
YOU'RE A HOT DOG
BUT YOU'D BETTER NOT TRY TO HURT HER
FRANK FURTER
MAGENTA
(On her own.)
YOU'RE A HOT DOG
BUT YOU'D BETTER NOT TRY TO HURT HER
FRANK FURTER

London cast.

(FRANK nods to RIFF RAFF who gives MAGENTA a liberal spraying. She purrs and collapses on to the Coke machine.)

FRANK

Columbia—the artistes are in a molecular state somewhere between entrance and exit. *(RIFF RAFF sprays COLUMBIA)* When they've pulled themselves together—see that they are prepared for the floorshow.

(COLUMBIA flips.)

COLUMBIA

(Speaking slowly at first, then getting faster and higher.)

Oh wow—I dig that—it's wicked, it's a gas—I'm groovy I'm hip, man—it's like a trip—ah, wow, my God—freak out baby—dig you later.

(COLUMBIA buzzes, jumps left, and exits. There is a pause.)

FRANK

It's not easy having a good time—even smiling makes my face ache—and my children turn on me—Rocky's behaving just as Eddie did—maybe I made a mistake in splitting his brain between the two of them.

(RIFF RAFF smiles and says nothing.)

Patricia Quinn (Magenta), London cast.

MAGENTA

(Crossing to FRANK, loudly.)

When do we return to Transylvania?—
I grow weary of this world.

FRANK

(Groaning as if he has a headache.)

Magenta, I am indeed grateful to both you and
your brother Riff Raff—you have both served me
well—loyalty such as yours must be rewarded,
and you will discover that when the mood takes me,
I can be quite generous.

(He strokes MAGENTA and puts his arm around her.)

MAGENTA

(Throws his arm off.)

I ask for nothing, Master.

FRANK

And you shall receive it in abundance.
Come—our guests will be growing restless.

(FRANK exits.)

*(MAGENTA and RIFF RAFF look at one another—
they make an extraterrestrial sign.)*

(Strobe light Blackout.)

Patricia Quinn (Magenta) and Richard O'Brien (Riff Raff), London cast.

THE
ROCKY
HORROR
SHOW

(A spotlight picks up the NARRATOR.)

NARRATOR

And so, by some extraordinary coincidence—fate it seems had decided that Brad and Janet should keep that appointment with their friend Dr. Evrett Scott. But, it was to be in a situation which none of them could have possibly foreseen. And, just a few hours after announcing their engagement Brad and Janet had both tasted forbidden fruit—this in itself was proof that their host was a man of little morals and some persuasion—What further indignities were they to be subjected to . . . ? And what of the sonic transducer and the floorshow that had been spoken of? What indeed? From what had gone before it was clear that this was to be no picnic.

Opposite: Jonathan Adams (Narrator). Following pages: London cast.

ROSE TINT MY WORLD

SCENE TEN

(Each enters singly through slash curtain—wearing black stockings and suspenders and black underwear and finally they become a chorus line.)

COLUMBIA

IT WAS GREAT
WHEN IT ALL BEGAN
I WAS A REGULAR FRANKY FAN
BUT IT WAS OVER WHEN HE HAD THE PLAN
TO START WORKING ON A MUSCLE-MAN
NOW THE ONLY THING THAT GIVES ME HOPE
IS MY LOVE OF A CERTAIN DOPE
ROSE TINTS MY WORLD KEEPS ME
SAFE FROM MY TROUBLE AND PAIN

(As ROCKY enters, COLUMBIA throws the microphone to him. COLUMBIA freezes stage left.)

ROCKY

I'M JUST SEVEN HOURS OLD
TRULY BEAUTIFUL TO BEHOLD
AND SOMEBODY SHOULD BE TOLD
MY LIBIDO HASN'T BEEN CONTROLLED
NOW THE ONLY THING I'VE COME TO TRUST
IS AN ORGASMIC RUSH OF LUST
ROSE TINTS MY WORLD KEEPS ME
SAFE FROM MY TROUBLE AND PAIN

(ROCKY throws the microphone to BRAD, then freezes stage right.)

BRAD

IT'S BEYOND ME
HELP ME MOMMY
I'LL BE GOOD YOU'LL SEE
TAKE THIS DREAM AWAY
WHAT'S THIS, LET'S SEE
I FEEL SEXY
WHAT'S COME OVER ME
HERE IT COMES AGAIN

Nell Campbell (Columbia), London cast.

London cast.

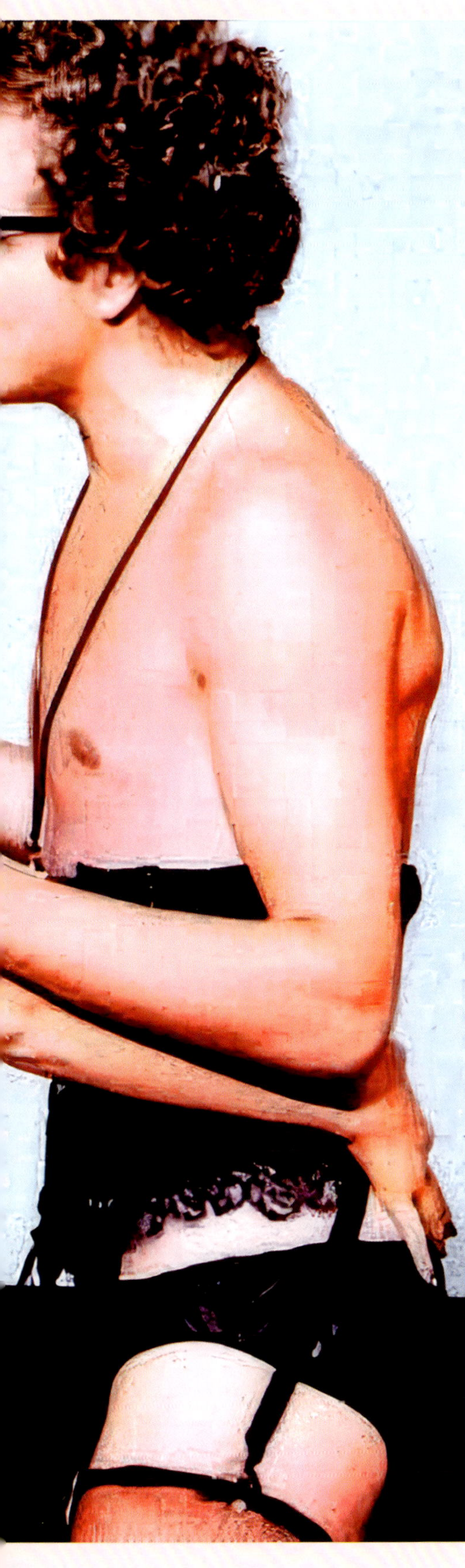

(ROCKY throws the microphone to BRAD, then freezes stage right.)

JANET

I FEEL RELEASED
BAD TIMES DECEASED
MY CONFIDENCE HAS INCREASED
REALITY IS HERE
THE GAME HAS BEEN DISBANDED
MY MIND HAS BEEN EXPANDED
IT'S A GAS THAT FRANKY'S LANDED
HIS LUST IS SO SINCERE

(Band plays fanfare.)

(PHANTOMS enter in similar costumes.)

(FRANK makes spectacular entrance.)

FRANK

WHATEVER HAPPENED TO FAY WRAY
THAT DELICATE SATIN DRAPED FRAME
AS IT CLUNG TO HER THIGH
HOW I STARTED TO CRY
FOR I WANTED TO BE DRESSED JUST THE SAME
GIVE YOURSELF OVER TO ABSOLUTE PLEASURE
SWIM THE WARM WATERS OF SINS OF THE FLESH
EROTIC NIGHTMARES BEYOND ANY MEASURE
AND SENSUAL DAYDREAMS TO TREASURE FOREVER—
CAN'T YOU JUST SEE IT
WHOA WHOA WHOA
(Spoken) Don't dream it—be it.

ALL *(Sung)*

DON'T DREAM IT—BE IT

(They all come together touching and fondling one another, FRANK in the center.)

DON'T DREAM IT—BE IT
DON'T DREAM IT—BE IT
DON'T DREAM IT—BE IT
DON'T DREAM IT—BE IT
DON'T DREAM IT—BE IT
DON'T DREAM IT—BE IT

(SCOTTY enters, speaks following over last 2 choruses above.)

SCOTTY

Hmm . . . We've got to get out of this trap
Before this decadence saps our wills
I've got to be strong and try to hang on
Or my mind may well snap
And my life will be lived

(SCOTTY removes his blanket, revealing stockings and high heels.)

(Sings)

FOR THE THRILLS

BRAD

IT'S BEYOND ME
HELP ME MOMMY

JANET

GOD BLESS LILY ST. CYR

FRANK

MY MY MY MY MY MY MY
MY MY MY MY MY MY MY

(They all form chorus line.)

I'M A WILD AND UNTAMED THING
I'M A BEE WITH A DEADLY STING
GET A HIT AND YOUR MIND GOES PING
YOUR HEART'LL THUMP
AND YOUR BLOOD WILL SING
SO LET THE PARTY AND THE SOUNDS ROCK ON
GONNA SHAKE IT TILL THE LIFE HAS GONE
ROSE TINT MY WORLD
KEEP ME SAFE FROM MY TROUBLE AND PAIN

ALL

WE'RE A WILD AND UNTAMED THING
WE ARE BEES WITH A DEADLY STING
GET A HIT AND YOUR MIND GOES PING
YOUR HEART'LL THUMP
AND YOUR BLOOD WILL SING
SO LET THE PARTY AND THE SOUNDS ROCK ON
GONNA SHAKE IT TILL THE LIFE HAS GONE
ROSE TINT MY WORLD
KEEP ME SAFE FROM MY TROUBLE AND PAIN
WE'RE A WILD AND UNTAMED THING
WE ARE BEES WITH A DEADLY STING
GET A HIT AND YOUR MIND GOES PING
YOUR HEART'LL THUMP
AND YOUR BLOOD WILL SING
SO LET THE PARTY AND THE SOUNDS ROCK ON
GONNA SHAKE IT TILL THE LIFE HAS GONE
ROSE TINT MY WORLD
KEEP ME SAFE FROM MY TROUBLE AND PAIN

(RIFF RAFF and MAGENTA enter dressed in extraterrestrial national costume.)

RIFF RAFF

FRANK N FURTER
IT'S ALL OVER
YOUR MISSION IS A FAILURE
YOUR LIFESTYLE'S TOO EXTREME
I'M YOUR NEW COMMANDER
YOU NOW ARE MY PRISONER
WE RETURN TO TRANSYLVANIA
PREPARE THE TRANSIT BEAM

(ALL freeze except MAGENTA who goes to do RIFF RAFF's bidding.)

FRANK

Wait—I can explain.

Los Angeles cast.

I'M GOING HOME

(FRANK arranges stage for next number.)

FRANK

ON THE DAY I WENT AWAY

ALL

GOODBYE

FRANK

WAS ALL I HAD TO SAY

ALL

NOW I

FRANK

WANT TO COME AGAIN AND STAY

ALL

OH MY MY

FRANK.

SMILE AND THAT WILL MEAN I MAY
I'VE SEEN BLUE SKIES
THROUGH THE TEARS IN MY EYES
AND I REALIZE I'M GOING HOME

ALL

I'M GOING HOME.

FRANK

EVERYWHERE IT'S BEEN THE SAME

ALL

FEELING

FRANK

LIKE I'M OUTSIDE IN THE RAIN

ALL

WHEELING

FRANK

FREE TO TRY AND FIND A GAME

ALL

DEALING

FRANK

CARDS FOR SORROW CARDS FOR PAIN
I'VE SEEN THE BLUE SKIES
THROUGH THE TEARS IN MY EYES
AND I REALIZE—I'M GOING HOME

ALL

I'M GOING HOME
I'M GOING HOME
(Song ends.)

Tim Curry (Frank-N-Furter), Los Angeles cast.

SCENE ELEVEN

MAGENTA

How sentimental.

RIFF RAFF

And also presumptuous of you—you see when I said 'we' were to return I referred only to Magenta and myself—I'm sorry however if you found my words misleading—you see you are to remain here—in spirit anyway—

(He produces a ray gun.)

SCOTTY

Great heavens—that's a laser.

RIFF RAFF

Yes, Dr. Scott, a laser capable of emitting a beam of pure anti-matter.

BRAD

You mean you're going to kill him?—What's his crime?

FRANK

Oh Brad.

SCOTTY

You saw what had become of Eddie—Society must be protected.

RIFF RAFF

Exactly, Dr. Scott—Now Frank-N-Furter, your time has come—say goodbye to all this—and hello to oblivion.

FRANK

Do your worst—inferior one.

COLUMBIA

No! No!

(COLUMBIA runs to shield FRANK, she is hit.)

FRANK

Did you do this for me?

Richard O'Brien (Riff Raff) and Patricia Quinn (Magenta), London cast.

(COLUMBIA throws herself between RIFF RAFF and FRANK—ZAPPP—COLUMBIA and FRANK are both killed. COLUMBIA dies quickly. FRANK enjoys it more.)

(ROCKY bellows, beats his chest, and picks up FRANK. RIFF RAFF fires again and again until finally ROCKY dies, spectacularly.)

BRAD

Good God.

RIFF RAFF

Yes.

JANET

You've killed them.

MAGENTA

I thought you liked them—they liked you.

RIFF RAFF

(Screaming)

They didn't like me—They never liked me. You saw the way things were—the way they were going.

SCOTTY

You did right.

(RIFF RAFF points gun at SCOTTY.)

Oh shit.

RIFF RAFF

A decision has to be made.

SCOTTY

You're O.K. by me.

RIFF RAFF

Dr. Scott I'm sorry about your nephew.

SCOTTY

Yes—Perhaps it's for the best.

RIFF RAFF

You should leave now, Dr. Scott,
while it is still possible.
We are about to beam the entire house
back to the planet of Transsexual.
Go now.

(BRAD pushes SCOTTY and JANET offstage. RIFF RAFF and MAGENTA look at one another. They start to laugh quietly. Their laughter builds as they climb to the laboratory and sit on the Coke fridge.)

MAGENTA

I wonder if I remembered to cancel the milk.

RIFF RAFF

No matter, Magenta—activate the transit crystal.

(There is a flash and a bang and RIFF RAFF and MAGENTA are gone. The introduction to "SUPER HEROES" starts. The cloud effect plays on the screen, then a spotlight picks up BRAD as he climbs up the ladder.)

SUPER HEROES

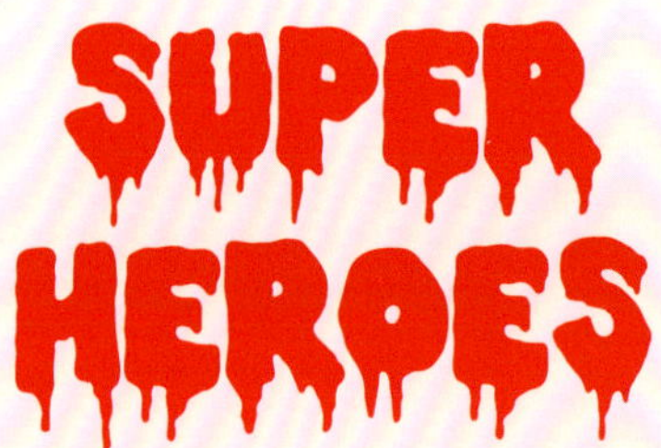

BRAD
I'VE DONE A LOT
GOD KNOWS I'VE TRIED
TO FIND THE TRUTH
I'VE EVEN LIED
BUT ALL I KNOW
IS DOWN INSIDE
PHANTOMS
I'M BLEEDING
(A light picks up JANET as she climbs up the ladder and sings.)
JANET
AND SUPER HEROES
COME TO FEAST
TO TASTE THE FLESH
NOT YET DECEASED
AND ALL I KNOW
IS STILL THE BEAST
PHANTOMS
IS FEEDING
(BRAD and JANET try to touch hands.)
AHHH AHHH
(Four times—Chant.)

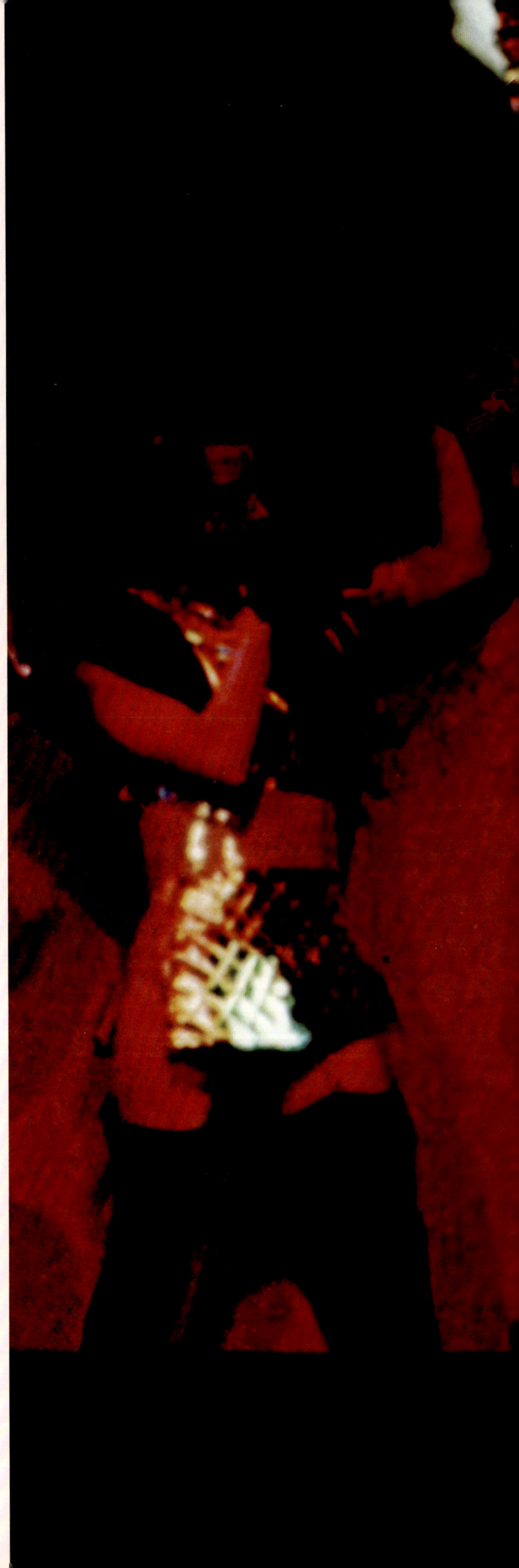

(The entire cast, except MAGENTA, come on stage in front of the screen. FRANK stands on the box.)
(The NARRATOR steps forward.)

NARRATOR

AND CRAWLING ON
THE PLANET'S FACE
SOME INSECTS CALLED
THE HUMAN RACE LOST IN TIME
AND LOST IN SPACE

PHANTOMS

AND MEANING

(There is a slow fade to black-out. The curtains close and MAGENTA comes between them as the USHERETTE.)

Graham Jarvis (Narrator), Los Angeles cast.

SCIENCE FICTION/ DOUBLE FEATURE (REPRISE)

EPILOGUE

USHERETTE

SCIENCE FICTION DOUBLE FEATURE
FRANK HAS BUILT AND LOST HIS CREATURE
DARKNESS HAS CONQUERED BRAD AND JANET
THE SERVANTS GONE TO A DISTANT PLANET
OH—AT THE LATE NIGHT DOUBLE FEATURE
PICTURE SHOW—I WANT TO GO—OHH—
TO THE LATE NIGHT DOUBLE FEATURE PICTURE SHOW
(NARRATOR'S voice.)
DO LANG DOO LANG

THE END
(Blackout)

Patricia Quinn (Usherette), London cast.

STRAWBERRY
TIME

THE VIRGIN'S GUIDE TO
THE ROCKY HORROR SHOW

Ever since the movie became a midnight show staple, audience participation was part of the fun of Rocky Horror. *Now, stage shows allow the audience to get in the fun too. So for all you (theater) virgins out there who want a leg up on what to do when you see the stage show, we present the full theatrical script with some of the globally used, tried-and-true favorite bits of audience participation.*

Prologue

SCIENCE FICTION/DOUBLE FEATURE

USHERETTE

MICHAEL RENNIE WAS ILL
THE DAY THE EARTH STOOD STILL
BUT HE TOLD US WHERE WE STAND
AND FLASH GORDON WAS THERE
IN SILVER UNDERWEAR
CLAUDE RAINS WAS THE INVISIBLE MAN
THEN SOMETHING WENT WRONG
FOR FAY WRAY AND KING KONG
THEY GOT CAUGHT IN A CELLULOID JAM
THEN AT A DEADLY PACE
IT CAME FROM OUTER SPACE
AND THIS IS HOW THE MESSAGE RAN.

(CHORUS)
SCIENCE FICTION—DOUBLE FEATURE
DR. X WILL BUILD A CREATURE
SEE ANDROIDS FIGHTING BRAD AND JANET
ANNE FRANCES STARS IN FORBIDDEN PLANET
OH—AT THE LATE NIGHT [What kind of feature?]
DOUBLE FEATURE [What kind of show?]
PICTURE SHOW.

I KNEW LEO G. CARROL
WAS OVER A BARREL
WHEN TARANTULA TOOK TO THE HILLS
AND I REALLY GOT HOT
WHEN I SAW JANETTE SCOTT
FIGHT A TRIFFID THAT SPITS POISON AND KILLS
DANA ANDREWS SAID PRUNES
GIVE HIM THE RHUNES
AND PASSING THEM USED LOTS OF SKILLS
AND WHEN WORLDS COLLIDE
SAID GEORGE PAL TO HIS BRIDE
I'M GOING TO GIVE YOU SOME TERRIBLE THRILLS
LIKE A—

(CHORUS)
SCIENCE FICTION—DOUBLE FEATURE
DR. X WILL BUILD A CREATURE
SEE ANDROIDS FIGHTING BRAD AND JANET
ANNE FRANCES STARS IN FORBIDDEN PLANET
OH—AT THE LATE NIGHT DOUBLE FEATURE
PICTURE SHOW.
I WANT TO GO
OH—AT THE LATE NIGHT [What kind of feature?]
DOUBLE FEATURE [What kind of show?] PICTURE SHOW
BY R.K.O.
OH—AT THE LATE NIGHT [What kind of feature?]
DOUBLE FEATURE [What kind of show?]
PICTURE SHOW
IN THE BACK ROW
OH—AT THE LATE NIGHT [What kind of feature?]
DOUBLE FEATURE [What kind of show?] PICTURE SHOW

Scene One

JANET

Oh Brad, wasn't it wonderful—didn't Betty look radiantly beautiful—I can't believe it—just an hour ago she was plain Betty Munroe and now she's Mrs. Ralf Hapshatt. [Half-Shit!]

BRAD

Yes, Janet—Ralf's a lucky guy.
[No he's not, she's got syph!]

JANET

Yes.

BRAD

Everyone knows Betty's a wonderful little cook.
[She's the hottest baked potato in Denton!]
[Yeah, Denton—the home of happiness!]

JANET

Yes.

BRAD

And Ralf himself will be in line for promotion in a year or two. [If he doesn't get busted!]

JANET

[Janet, are you a slut?] Yes, Brad.

DAMMIT, JANET

BRAD

HEY, JANET.

JANET

YES BRAD.

BRAD

I'VE GOT SOMETHING TO SAY. [Then say it!]

JANET

YES.

BRAD

I REALLY LOVED THE [starts with an s] SKILLFUL
WAY [what a genius!]
YOU BEAT THE OTHER GIRLS [with a whip]
TO THE BRIDE'S BOUQUET.

THE RIVER WAS DEEP BUT I SWAM IT.
THE FUTURE IS OURS SO LET'S PLAN IT.
SO PLEASE DON'T TELL ME TO CAN IT.
I'VE ONE THING TO SAY AND THAT'S . . .
DAMN IT—JANET—I LOVE YOU.
THE ROAD WAS LONG BUT I RAN IT.
THERE'S A FIRE IN MY HEART AND YOU FAN IT.
IF THERE'S A FOOL FOR YOU THEN I AM IT.
I'VE ONE THING TO SAY AND THAT'S
DAMN IT—JANET—I LOVE YOU.
HERE'S A RING TO PROVE I'M NO JOKER
(Bell voices.)
THERE'S THREE WAYS THAT LOVE CAN GROW
THAT'S GOOD—BAD—OR MEDIOCRE
J-A-N-E-T
I LOVE YOU SO.

JANET

OH IT'S NICER THAN BETTY MUNROE HAD.
NOW WE'RE ENGAGED AND I'M SO GLAD.
THAT YOU'VE MET MOM AND YOU KNOW DAD.
I'VE ONE THING TO SAY AND THAT'S . . .
BRAD—I'M MAD—FOR YOU TOO.
OH BRAD.

BRAD

OH DAMN IT.

JANET

I'M MAD.

BRAD

OH JANET.

JANET

FOR YOU.

BRAD

I LOVE YOU TOO—THERE'S ONE THING LEFT
TO DO AND THAT'S . . .
GO SEE THE MAN THAT BEGAN IT
WHEN WE MET IN HIS SCIENCE EXAM IT
MADE ME GIVE YOU THE EYE AND THEN PANIC
NOW I'VE ONE THING TO SAY AND THAT'S . . .
DAMN IT—JANET—I LOVE YOU.
DAMN IT JANET.

JANET

OH BRAD I'M MAD.

BRAD

DAMN IT JANET.

BRAD AND JANET

I LOVE YOU.

NARRATOR

I would like [you would, would you?]—if I may [you may]—to take you on a strange journey. [How strange was it?] It seemed a fairly ordinary night when Brad Majors, [asshole!] and his fiancée Janet Weiss [slut!]. . . *(two young ordinary healthy kids)* . . . left Denton that late November evening to visit a Dr. Evrett Scott [Snott!] ex tutor and now friend to both of them . . . [Is it true that you fuck sheep?] Its true there were dark storm clouds, [Describe your balls!] heavy—black and pendulous—toward which they were—driving, its true also that the spare tire they were carrying was badly in need of some air [like your fucking neck!]—but they being normal kids [normal?] and on a night out—well—they were not going to let a storm spoil the events of their evening. On a night out. [Come a little bit closer, Chucky.] *(Thunder)* It was a night out they were to remember [For how long?] *(Thunder)* for a very—long—time.

Scene Two

(Sound of a car approaching through a stormy night.)
(Headlights)
(Car stops.)

BRAD

Hmmm.

JANET

What's the matter, Brad darling?

BRAD

I think we took the wrong fork a few miles back there. [HUM TWILIGHT ZONE THEME SONG.] We'd better go on ahead up the road and see if we can find our way back. [Don't back up!]
(They move off. BLOW-OUT.)
Oh darn! Janet.

JANET
What was that bang?
BRAD
We seem to have a blow-out in the front left-hand tire.
JANET
Oh . . .
(Pause. Lightning and thunder.)
BRAD
You'd better stay here and keep warm while I go for help.
JANET
But where will you go? We're in the middle of nowhere.
BRAD
[Try the castle!] Didn't we pass a castle back down the road a few miles? [CHEER.] Maybe they have a telephone I might use.
JANET
I'm coming with you. [That'll be a first!]
BRAD
There's no point in both of us getting wet. [She's already wet!]
JANET
I'm coming with you. Besides, darling, the owner of the phone may be a beautiful woman, [He is!] and you may never come back. [You should be so lucky!]
BRAD
Ha Ha Ha.
[NEWSPAPERS OVER HEADS, SQUIRT THE VIRGINS SITTING IN FRONT OF YOU.]

OVER AT THE FRANKENSTEIN PLACE

[WAVE YOUR LIGHTS]
JANET
IN THE VELVET DARKNESS
OF THE BLACKEST NIGHT
BURNING BRIGHT—THERE'S A GUIDING STAR
NO MATTER WHAT OR WHO YOU ARE.
BRAD & JANET
THERE'S A LIGHT
PHANTOMS
OVER AT THE FRANKENSTEIN PLACE
BRAD & JANET
THERE'S A LIGHT
PHANTOMS
BURNING IN THE FIREPLACE
JANET
THERE'S A LIGHT . . . LIGHT IN THE DARKNESS OF EVERYBODY'S LIFE
BRAD
I CAN SEE THE FLAG FLY
I CAN SEE THE RAIN
JUST THE SAME—THERE HAS GOT TO BE
SOMETHING BETTER HERE—FOR YOU AND ME.
BRAD & JANET
THERE'S A LIGHT
PHANTOMS
OVER AT THE FRANKENSTEIN PLACE
BRAD & JANET
THERE'S A LIGHT
PHANTOMS
BURNING IN THE FIREPLACE
BRAD
THERE'S A LIGHT . . . LIGHT IN THE DARKNESS OF EVERYBODY'S LIFE
RIFF RAFF
THE DARKNESS MUST GO
DOWN THE RIVER OF NIGHTS DREAMING
FLOW MORPHIA SLOW LET THE SUN AND LIGHT
COME STREAMING INTO MY LIFE
INTO MY LIFE
JANET & BRAD
THERE'S A LIGHT
PHANTOMS
OVER AT THE FRANKENSTEIN PLACE
JANET & BRAD
THERE'S A LIGHT
PHANTOMS
BURNING IN THE FIREPLACE
THERE'S A LIGHT—LIGHT
JANET & BRAD
IN THE DARKNESS OF EVERYBODY'S LIFE
(Lightning)
JANET
Screams.
BRAD
It's all right, Janet.
JANET
Oh Brad let's go back. I'm cold and I'm frightened.
BRAD
Just a moment, Janet, they may have a telephone.
(PHANTOMS enter—mime a door.)
[Ding dong, asshole calling!]
(He rings the bell . . . No answer . . . Rings again . . . At last the door opens.)
(Door creak.)
RIFF RAFF
[Say hello, Riff.] Hello.
BRAD
Oh: Uh: Ahh: Hi there, we're in a bit of a spot, I wonder could you help us—our car is broken

down about two miles back do you have a telephone we might use?

RIFF RAFF

(Pause)

You're wet. [No shit, Sherlock!]

JANET

[Janet, are you a slut?] Yes—[Why?] the rain has been very heavy. [You're a slut because it's raining?]

BRAD

[Brad, are you an asshole?] Yes.

RIFF RAFF

[Riff, are you on drugs?] Yes—

(Lightning and Thunder.)

I think you better both come inside.

JANET

You're too kind.

RIFF RAFF

(Mimics JANET.)

You're too kind.

(Shuts door.)

(Blackout.)

NARRATOR

And so—after braving the inclement weather, and some not too little time—it seemed that fortune had smiled on Brad and Janet and that they had found the assistance that their plight required—or had they?—There was certainly something about this house (to which, a flat tire and a wet night had brought them) that made the both of them uneasy—but, if they were to reach their destination that night, they would have to ignore such feelings and take advantage of whatever help was offered.

Scene Three

RIFF RAFF

Wait here.

BRAD

(To RIFF RAFF as he exits.) Excuse me.

JANET

(Looking around.) Oh Brad what sort of a place is this—I'm frightened.

BRAD

It's probably some sort of hunting lodge for rich weirdos [Yay! Rich weirdos!]—but you're shivering.

JANET

Yes, I'm wet.

BRAD

Look, feel this—there's hot air coming from this grille in the wall—take off your sweater and dry it here. I'll keep a look out for the undertaker.

JANET

(Screams as sweater is snatched from her by hand through grill.) Oh!

BRAD

For God's sake keep a grip on yourself Janet. I'm here—there's nothing to worry about. *(She smiles.)* Here, dry my coat too.

JANET

O.K.

(RIFF RAFF, COLUMBIA and MAGENTA enter. JANET screams.) Agghhh!!!

BRAD

It's alright, Janet. Excuse me, hi, look if I could just use your phone, we'll move right along—I'm sure you've got a lot of things to do and a great evening planned.

RIFF RAFF

Oh yes, you've arrived on a rather special night, the master is having one of his affairs. [Which one?] [Don't say the magic word, Janet.]

JANET

Lucky old him.

MAGENTA

Yeah he's lucky—I'm lucky—you're lucky—we're all lucky . . . [We're all lucky!]

COLUMBIA

All except Eddie.

RIFF RAFF

SSHHH!!!

JANET

Eddie?

RIFF RAFF & MAGENTA

SSHHH!!!

MAGENTA

The delivery boy.

COLUMBIA

His delivery wasn't good enough.

RIFF RAFF

The master only wanted to help the boy better his position.

BRAD

That's very commendable . . .

RIFF RAFF

Yes, it seems like only yesterday since he went . . .

JANET

Where?

MAGENTA

To pieces.

RIFF RAFF & MAGENTA

Ha Ha Ha.

TIME WARP

[GET IN THE AISLE AND CROUCH DOWN.]

RIFF RAFF.

IT'S ASTOUNDING—TIME IS FLEETING [What's your favorite rock group?]

MADNESS [They suck!] TAKES IT'S TOLL [Fifty cents, please.]

BUT LISTEN CLOSELY—

MAGENTA & COLUMBIA.

NOT FOR VERY MUCH LONGER

RIFF RAFF.

I'VE GOT TO KEEP CONTROL

I REMEMBER DOING THE TIME WARP

DRINKING THOSE MOMENTS WHEN

THE BLACKNESS WOULD HIT ME—

AND THE VOID WOULD BE CALLING

[GET UP AND TIME WARP!]

ALL.

LET'S DO THE TIME WARP AGAIN

LET'S DO THE TIME WARP AGAIN

[How's it done?]

(CHORUS)

NARRATOR. *(MR. BASSMAN)*

IT'S JUST A JUMP TO THE LEFT

ALL.

AND THEN A STEP TO THE RIGHT

NARRATOR.

WITH YOUR HANDS ON YOUR HIPS

ALL.

YOU BRING YOUR KNEES IN TIGHT

BUT IT'S THE PELVIC THRUST

THAT STARTS TO DRIVE YOU INSANE

LET'S DO THE TIME WARP AGAIN

LET'S DO THE TIME WARP AGAIN

MAGENTA.

IT'S SO DREAMY—OH FANTASY FREE ME

SO YOU CAN'T SEE ME—NO NOT AT ALL

IN ANOTHER DIMENSION—WITH VOYEURISTIC INTENTION

WELL SECLUDED—I'LL SEE ALL

WITH A BIT OF A MIND FLIP—YOU'RE THERE IN THE TIME SLIP

NOTHING CAN EVER BE THE SAME

YOU'RE SPACED OUT ON SENSATION

RIFF RAFF & MAGENTA.

LIKE YOU'RE UNDER SEDATION

ALL.

LET'S DO THE TIME WARP AGAIN

LET'S DO THE TIME WARP AGAIN

[How's it done?]

(CHORUS)

NARRATOR. *(MR. BASSMAN)*

IT'S JUST A JUMP TO THE LEFT

ALL.

AND THEN A STEP TO THE RIGHT

NARRATOR.

WITH YOUR HANDS ON YOUR HIPS

ALL.

YOU BRING YOUR KNEES IN TIGHT

BUT IT'S THE PELVIC THRUST

THAT STARTS TO DRIVE YOU INSANE

LET'S DO THE TIME WARP AGAIN

LET'S DO THE TIME WARP AGAIN

COLUMBIA.

WELL I WAS WALKING DOWN THE STREET

JUST HAVING A THINK

WHEN A SNAKE OF A GUY GAVE ME AN EVIL WINK

WELL IT SHOOK ME UP, IT TOOK ME BY SURPRISE

HE HAD A PICK UP TRUCK AND THE DEVIL'S EYES

OH—HE STARED AT ME AND I FELT A CHANGE

TIME MEANT NOTHING—NEVER WOULD AGAIN

ALL.

LET'S DO THE TIME WARP AGAIN

LET'S DO THE TIME WARP AGAIN

(COLUMBIA—Tap break.)

LET'S DO THE TIME WARP AGAIN

LET'S DO THE TIME WARP AGAIN

[How's it done?]

(CHORUS)

NARRATOR. *(MR. BASSMAN)*

IT'S JUST A JUMP TO THE LEFT

ALL.

AND THEN A STEP TO THE RIGHT

NARRATOR.

WITH YOUR HANDS ON YOUR HIPS

ALL.

YOU BRING YOUR KNEES IN TIGHT

BUT IT'S THE PELVIC THRUST

THAT STARTS TO DRIVE YOU INSANE

LET'S DO THE TIME WARP AGAIN

LET'S DO THE TIME WARP AGAIN

(Song ends. RIFF RAFF, MAGENTA, COLUMBIA move menacingly toward BRAD and JANET.)

JANET

Say something Brad. [Say something, stupid asshole!]

BRAD

Ah . . . say, do you guys know how to Madison? [I do the Rock, myself.] Janet—out, out, step touch, step touch.

(Beat to "Sweet Transvestite.")

(RIFF RAFF, MAGENTA, COLUMBIA and PHANTOMS break off and prepare for entrance.)

JANET
Brad, let's get out of here, it seems so unhealthy here—I want to go.
BRAD
Well we can't go anywhere until I get to a phone.
JANET
This isn't the junior Chamber of Commerce Brad.
BRAD
They're probably foreigners with ways different to our own, they may do some more folk dancing.
JANET
Look I'm cold, I'm wet and I'm just plain scared.
BRAD
I'm here Janet, there's nothing to worry about.
(FRANK appears.)

SWEET TRANSVESTITE

FRANK
HOW DO YOU DO
I SEE YOU'VE MET MY FAITHFUL HANDYMAN
HE'S A LITTLE BROUGHT DOWN
BECAUSE WHEN YOU KNOCKED
HE THOUGHT YOU WERE THE CANDYMAN
(Spoken) Didn't you, Freaky.
DON'T GET STRUNG OUT BY THE WAY THAT I LOOK
DON'T JUDGE A BOOK BY IT'S COVER
I'M NOT MUCH OF A MAN
BY THE LIGHT OF DAY
BUT BY NIGHT I'M ONE HELL OF A LOVER
[CHEER, SCREAM, BOW DOWN IN PRAISE, ETC.]
I'M JUST A SWEET TRANSVESTITE
FROM TRANSSEXUAL
TRANSYLVANIA.
LET ME SHOW YOU AROUND, MAYBE PLAY YOU A SOUND
YOU LOOK LIKE YOU'RE BOTH PRETTY GROOVIE
OR IF YOU WANT SOMETHING VISUAL THAT'S NOT
TOO ABYSMAL
WE COULD TAKE IN AN OLD STEVE REEVES MOVIE
BRAD
I'M GLAD WE CAUGHT YOU AT HOME
AH—COULD WE USE YOUR PHONE
WE'RE BOTH IN A BIT OF A HURRY
WE'LL JUST SAY WHERE WE ARE
THEN GO BACK TO THE CAR [Fuck in the car!]
WE DON'T WANT TO BE ANY WORRY
FRANK
YOU GOT CAUGHT WITH A FLAT
WELL HOW ABOUT THAT
WELL BABIES DON'T YOU PANIC
BY THE LIGHT OF THE NIGHT
IT'LL ALL SEEM ALRIGHT
I'LL GET YOU A SATANIC MECHANIC
I'M JUST A
SWEET TRANSVESTITE
FROM TRANSSEXUAL
TRANSYLVANIA
WHY DON'T CHA STAY FOR THE NIGHT
RIFF RAFF, MAGENTA & COLUMBIA
NIGHT
FRANK
OR MAYBE A BITE
RIFF RAFF, MAGENTA & COLUMBIA
BITE
FRANK
I COULD SHOW YOU MY FAVOURITE OBSESSION [Sex!]
I'VE BEEN MAKING A MAN [You call that a man?]
WITH BLOND HAIR AND A TAN
AND HE'S GOOD FOR RELIEVING MY [Sexual!] TENSION
I'M JUST A SWEET TRANSVESTITE
FROM TRANSSEXUAL
TRANSYLVANIA
RIFF RAFF, MAGENTA & COLUMBIA
HIT IT, HIT IT
FRANK
I'M JUST A
SWEET TRANSVESTITE
FROM TRANSSEXUAL
TRANSYLVANIA
SO COME UP TO THE LAB
AND SEE WHAT'S ON THE SLAB
I SEE YOU SHIVER IN ANTICI—[Say it!]—PATION
BUT MAYBE THE RAIN
IS REALLY TO BLAME
SO I'LL REMOVE THE CAUSE [But what about the symptom?]
BUT NOT THE SYMPTOM

(FRANK exits. The SERVANTS undress JANET and BRAD. They are reduced to '50s underwear.)
BRAD
(Aside to JANET.) It's all right, Janet, everything's gonna be all right, we'll just play along for now—and we'll pull out the aces when the time is right. [Nice aces!]
JANET
This is no time for card tricks, Brad, are you sure we'll be alright?
MAGENTA
(Snatches JANET's bag.) No bags.
BRAD
I'm sure, Janet. *(To COLUMBIA, MAGENTA and RIFF RAFF.)* Uh. Hi there—I'm Brad Majors, this is Janet Weiss—my fiancée—[Brad, spell "urinate" in shorthand.] You are . . . [Close enough.]

COLUMBIA
You're very lucky to be invited up to Frank's laboratory, a lot of people would give their right arm for the privilege. [Or their left tit!]
BRAD
People like you maybe.
COLUMBIA
I've seen it.
JANET
Is he . . . is Frank . . . your husband?
RIFF RAFF
The master is not yet married, nor do I think ever will be—we are simply his [Slaves!] servants.
(RIFF RAFF exits with their clothes.)
(FRANK enters.)

Scene Four

FRANK
Unlock a mind—unmind a lock—its the same as the beginning of the end—do you follow?
JANET
No.
BRAD
It's an anagram, Janet.
FRANK
I wonder may I offer you something refreshing?
BRAD & JANET
No.
FRANK
No. You're right, I won't—how delightful to have fresh faces around. Magenta—Columbia—go and assist Riff Raff—I will entertain Ahh.
BRAD
Brad Majors.
FRANK
Brad Majors.
BRAD
And this is my fiancée Janet Weiss. *(He pronounces it "Vice.")*
FRANK
Weiss.
BRAD
Weiss.
FRANK
Enchanted. How nice—and what charming under-clothes you both have—but here, put these on. [And take those off.] (He hands JANET a lab coat and helps BRAD on with his, during speech.) They'll make you feel less [Naked?] vulnerable. [Same thing.] We don't often receive visitors here, let alone show them hospitality . . . [Horse brutality.]
BRAD
Hospitality! [Horse brutality?] All we wanted was to use your phone, a reasonable request which you have chosen to ignore.
JANET
Don't be ungrateful, Brad.
BRAD
Ungrateful!
FRANK
How forceful you are, Brad, what a perfect example of manhood—so [Big.] dominant [BREAK OUT INTO A FLURRY OF LAUGHTER.]—you must be very proud, Janet.
JANET
[Janet, are you a slut?] Yes.
FRANK
Tell me Brad, do you have any tattoos?
BRAD
[Show him the teddy bear!] Certainly not.
FRANK
Oh well . . . [Ask Janet.]
(To JANET.)
How about you?
(Enter RIFF RAFF.)
RIFF RAFF
Everything is in readiness, Master. [Bater.] We merely wait for you to give the word.
FRANK
[Hey, Frank, when's the orgy and who's invited?]
Tonight Brad and Janet, you are to witness a new breakthrough in Biochemical [Bisexual!] research and paradise is [A garage!] to be mine . . .
JANET
Oh how wonderful for you.
FRANK
Yes. It was strange the way it happened . . . one of those quirks of fate really . . . one of those moments when . . . everything looks black, the chips are down, your back is against the wall. You panic—you're trapped—there's no way out and even if there was it would probably be a one way ticket to the bottom of the bay. And then suddenly you get a break—all the pieces seem to fit into place [Like a puzzle?]—what a sucker you'd been—what a fool—the answer was there all the time—it took a small accident to make it happen. [What was, your birth?]
(All look at FRANK in amazement.)
An accident.
MAGENTA & COLUMBIA
An accident.
[PREPARE NOISEMAKERS.]

FRANK

That's how I discovered the secret—that elusive ingredient—that spark that is the breath of life. Yes. I have that knowledge, [What do you hold between your legs?] I hold the key to life itself, [F!] you see [K!] Brad and Janet you are fortunate for tonight is the night my beautiful creature is destined to be [Blown!] born. Throw open the switches on the Sonic Oscillator [Oscillator? I just met her!] and step up the Reactor Power Input . . . three more points. [Three more triangles!]

(The lab has a series of mechanisms that can be changed according to its design.)

(The lab lights up in stages throughout the following.)

JANET

Brad!

BRAD

[How's your sex life, Brad?] It's alright Janet.

FRANK

Balls.

(3 Chords.)

JANET

Brad!

BRAD

It's alright Janet.

FRANK

Tubes.

(3 Chords.)

JANET

Brad!

BRAD

It's alright Janet.

FRANK

Crimps.

(3 Chords.)

(ROCKY is revealed in swaddling clothes.)(FRANK disrobes him during the song.)

THE SWORD OF DAMOCLES

ROCKY

THE SWORD OF DAMOCLES IS HANGING OVER MY HEAD
AND I'VE GOT THE FEELING SOMEONE IS GONNA
BE CUTTING
THE THREAD
OH WHO IS ME—MY LIFE IS A MISERY
OH CAN'T YOU SEE I'M AT THE START
OF A PRETTY BIG DOWNER
I WOKE UP THIS MORNING WITH A START WHEN
I FELL OUT OF THE BED

ALL

THAT AIN'T NO CRIME

ROCKY

AND LEFT FROM MY DREAMING WAS A FEELING
OF UNAMIABLE DREAD

ALL

THAT AIN'T NO CRIME

ROCKY

MY HIGH IS LOW—I'M DRESSED UP WITH NO PLACE
TO GO AND ALL I KNOW IS I'M AT THE
START OF A PRETTY BIG DOWNER

ALL

(SHA LA LA LA THAT AIN'T NO CRIME)
(SHA LA LA LA THAT AIN'T NO CRIME)
(SHA LA LA LA THAT AIN'T NO CRIME)
(THAT AIN'T NO CRIME)

NARRATOR

ROCKY HORROR YOU NEED PEACE OF MIND—AND I
WANT TO TELL YOU THAT YOU'RE DOING JUST FINE
YOU'RE THE PRODUCT OF ANOTHER TIME AND
FEELING DOWN WELL THAT'S NO CRIME

ALL

THAT AIN'T NO CRIME

ROCKY

THE SWORD OF DAMOCLES IS HANGING OVER MY HEAD

ALL

THAT AIN'T NO CRIME

ROCKY

AND I'VE GOT THE FEELING THAT SOMEONE'S GOING TO
BE
CUTTING THE THREAD

ALL

THAT AIN'T NO CRIME

ROCKY

OH WOE IS ME—MY LIFE IS A MYSTERY
OH CAN'T YOU SEE THAT I'M AT THE START
OF A PRETTY BIG DOWNER

ALL

SHA LA LA LA THAT AIN'T NO CRIME
SHA LA LA LA THAT AIN'T NO CRIME
SHA LA LA LA THAT AIN'T NO CRIME
THAT AIN'T NO CRIME
SHA LA LA LA THAT AIN'T NO CRIME
SHA LA LA LA THAT AIN'T NO CRIME
(SHA LA LA LA THAT AIN'T NO CRIME)
THAT AIN'T NO CRIME
SHA LA LA

FRANK

Well really [No, Frankly!]—that's no way to behave on your first day out. [Of the closet!]

ROCKY
Well nobody's perfect—But I do think you made a pretty good job of the body work.
FRANK
You are the result of many hours of toil—and now my beautiful creature you're ready for the ultimate test.
ROCKY
Oh dear.
FRANK
But first meet the family. Well Riff Raff what do you think?
RIFF RAFF
He's a credit to my/your genius.
FRANK
Magenta?
MAGENTA
A triumph of the will.
FRANK
What do you think Columbia?
COLUMBIA
He's OK. [You blew it, bitch!]
FRANK
OK! I think we can do better than that. [Ask Ken and Barbie!] Well, Brad and Janet, what do you think? [Lie through your teeth, Janet!]
JANET
I don't like men with too many muscles. [Just one BIG one!]
FRANK
I didn't make him for you. [Yeah, but she gets him anyway!] He carries the Charles Atlas seal of approval. [And he didn't even take the lessons!] [CLAP AND BARK LIKE A SEAL.] Maestro . . . [PREPARE YOUR CONFETTI.]

I CAN MAKE YOU A MAN

A WEAKLING WEIGHING 98 POUNDS
GETS SAND IN HIS FACE WHEN KICKED
TO THE GROUND
AND SOON IN THE GYM
WITH A DETERMINED CHIN
THE SWEAT FROM HIS PORES
AS HE WORKS FOR HIS CAUSE
WILL MAKE HIM GLISTEN AND GLEAM
AND WITH MASSAGE AND JUST A BIT OF STEAM
HE'LL BE PINK BUT QUITE CLEAN
HE'LL BE A STRONG MAN
ALL
BUT THE WRONG MAN
FRANK
HE'LL EAT NUTRITIOUS HIGH-PROTEIN
AND SWALLOW RAW EGGS
TRY TO BUILD UP HIS SHOULDERS
CHEST, ARMS AND LEGS
SUCH AN EFFORT
IF ONLY HE KNEW OF MY PLAN
WHEN IN JUST SEVEN DAYS
I CAN MAKE YOU A MAN
HE'LL DO PRESS UPS AND CHIN UPS
THE SNATCH CLEAN AND JERK
DYNAMIC TENSION
MUST BE AWFULLY HARD WORK
SUCH STRENUOUS LIVING
I JUST DON'T UNDERSTAND
WHEN IN JUST SEVEN DAYS
I CAN MAKE YOU A MAN
COLUMBIA
Eddie!
(A Coke machine is revealed. EDDIE is inside.)
HOT PATOOTIE
[THROW YOUR CONFETTI AS EDDIE COMES OUT.]
EDDIE
WHATEVER HAPPENED TO SATURDAY NIGHT
WHEN YOU DRESSED UP SHARP AND YOU FELT ALRIGHT
IT DON'T SEEM THE SAME SINCE COSMIC LIGHT
CAME INTO MY LIFE AND I THOUGHT I WAS DIVINE
I USED TO GO FOR A RIDE WITH A CHICK WHO'D GO
AND LISTEN TO THE MUSIC ON THE RADIO
A SAXOPHONE WAS BLOWING ON A ROCK AND ROLL SHOW
AND YOU CLIMBED IN THE BACK AND YOU REALLY HAD
A GOOD TIME
ALL
HOT PATOOTIE BLESS MY SOUL
I REALLY LOVE THAT ROCK AND ROLL
HOT PATOOTIE BLESS MY SOUL
I REALLY LOVE THAT ROCK AND ROLL
HOT PATOOTIE BLESS MY SOUL
I REALLY LOVE THAT ROCK AND ROLL
HOT PATOOTIE BLESS MY SOUL
I REALLY LOVE THAT ROCK AND ROLL
EDDIE
MY HEAD USED TO SWIM FROM THE PERFUME I SMELT
MY HANDS KIND OF FUMBLED WITH HER WHITE PLASTIC BELT
I'D TASTE HER BABY PINK LIPSTICK AND THAT'S WHEN I'D MELT
AND SHE'D WHISPER IN MY EAR TONIGHT SHE REALLY WAS MINE
GET BACK IN FRONT AND PUT SOME HAIR OIL ON
BUDDY HOLLY WAS SINGING HIS VERY LAST SONG
WITH YOUR ARM ROUND YOUR GIRL YOU'D TRY TO SING ALONG

YOU FELT PRETTY GOOD 'CAUSE YOU'D REALLY HAD
A GOOD TIME

ALL

HOT PATOOTIE BLESS MY SOUL
I REALLY LOVE THAT ROCK AND ROLL
REPEAT 7X

(EDDIE is forced back into container. FRANK kills him violently. (COLUMBIA is distraught.)

FRANK

One from the vaults.
(He transforms her mood.) [PREPARE YOUR RICE.]
Columbia . . .

ROCKY

Why do you keep him in there? He's so ugly.

FRANK

A certain naïve charm. But no muscle. We had a mental relationship—

FRANK

BUT A DELTOID AND A BICEP
A HOT GROIN AND A TRICEP
MAKES ME SHAKE
MAKES ME WANT TO TAKE
CHARLES ATLAS BY THE HAND

PHANTOMS

IN JUST SEVEN DAYS I CAN MAKE YOU A MAN

FRANK

I DON'T WANT NO DISSENSION
JUST DYNAMIC TENSION

JANET

I'M A MUSCLE FAN

ALL

IN JUST SEVEN DAYS I CAN MAKE YOU A MAN

FRANK

DIG IN IF YOU CAN

ALL

IN JUST SEVEN DAYS I CAN MAKE YOU A MAN

(Band plays "WEDDING MARCH." MAGENTA and COLUMBIA give FRANK a bouquet and veil. PHANTOMS throw confetti.)

[THROW YOUR RICE.]

(Wedding procession takes place. FRANK throws the bouquet. RIFF RAFF catches it.)

END OF ACT I

ACT II

ENTR'ACT

NARRATOR

Welcome back, *(Insert City.)*. Do pay attention. There are those who say life is an illusion—And reality as we know it, is merely a figment of our imaginations. If this is so, Brad and Janet are quite safe. [With their necks.] But—there are some who have a far more physical philosophy—those who would stop at nothing to satisfy their base desires—It could be that Brad and Janet are among those who hold the devil's reins.

Scene Five

JANET'S ROOM.

JANET

Oh Brad—Oh Yes—Yes my darling—What if—

BRAD

It's all right Janet [I've got a condom.]—everything's going to be all right. [Don't fuck with the hair!]

JANET

Oh I hope so my darling. I'm so fri . . . *(Lights up. Scene played in silhouette.)* You! [We told you not to fuck with the hair!]

FRANK

I'm afraid so, Janet. But wasn't it nice . . .

JANET

You beast—you monster—what have you done with Brad?

FRANK

Mmm—nothing—[He's saving the best for last!] why, do you think I should?

JANET

You tricked me—I wouldn't have—I've never—Oh my God—never. [What about the football team?] [That was just practice.] *(FRANK removes condom and throws it away.)*

FRANK

I know—but it wasn't all bad, was it? [It wasn't all Brad, either!] Not really even half bad—in fact, I think perhaps you found it quite—pleasurable—Mmm—so soft so—sensual.

JANET

Ahh—no—stop—I mean help—I—Brad—Ohhh—Brad. [He's not down there! He's never been down there.]

FRANK

Shh. Brad's probably asleep by now—do you want him to see you like this?

JANET

Like this? Like how?

FRANK

Like this.

JANET

It's your fault, you're to blame [No, Sue's to blame!] . . . I was saving myself. [For what, a rainy day? Look outside, bitch—it's pouring!]

FRANK

Well I'm sure you're not spent yet [Go ahead, spend her. I have change for a nickel.] and it

was an enjoyable experience was it not?
(Lights dim.)
You did like it, didn't you? There's no crime in giving yourself over to pleasure—is there? We could try for an action replay—Oh Janet you've wasted so much time already—Brad needn't know. I won't tell him, Mmmm.
(Blackout)
JANET
Are you sure you won't tell him? Ohhh . . .

Scene Six

BRAD'S ROOM
[Rocky Horror sex scene, take two!]
JANET
Oh Brad—Oh yes—Yes my darling, but what if . . .
BRAD
Its all right Janet everything's going to be all right.
JANET
I hope so my darling. [Don't fuck with the hair!]
(Lights up.)
(Scene played in silhouette.)
BRAD
You!
FRANK
I'm afraid so Brad—but wasn't it nice . . .
BRAD
You fiend, you scoundrel—What have you done with Janet?
FRANK
Mmm—nothing—why, do you think I should? [Again?]
BRAD
You tricked me, I wouldn't have—I've never [Never never? What about the Boy Scout troops?]—Oh my God—never.
(FRANK removes condom from BRAD.)
FRANK
I know—but it wasn't all bad was it? [It's all Brad this time.] Not really even half bad, in fact, I think you found it quite pleasurable—Oh so soft—so sensual.
BRAD
Ah—Help—No—stop. I mean—[Poke him in the eye!] Janet—Ohh—Janet. [She's not down there! She's never been down there!]
FRANK
Shh—Janet's probably asleep by now—Do you want her to see you like this?
BRAD
Like this like how—
FRANK
Like this. [Assume the position.]
BRAD
It's your fault. You're to blame—I thought it was the real thing. [It is, only bigger!]
FRANK
Oh come on Brad admit it. It was enjoyable wasn't it? You liked it didn't you? There's no crime in giving yourself over to pleasure [There is in New Jersey.]—is there?
(Lights dim.)
We could try for an action replay. Oh Brad you've wasted so much time already—Janet needn't know. I won't tell her—Mmm . . .
(Blackout)
BRAD
Are you sure you won't tell her—Ohhh . . .
RIFF RAFF
(On intercom.)
Master—The laboratory is empty. Rocky has vanished [Poof!]—the new playmate is loose and somewhere in the building.
FRANK
Oh—Wow—What a—Mmm—Oh—Coming.

Scene Seven

LABORATORY
JANET
What's happening here—Where's Brad?—Where's anybody? If only we hadn't made this journey [But you did!]—if only the car hadn't broken down [But it did!]—if only we were amongst friends [But you're not!] or sane persons. [Two out of three ain't bad!]

NARRATOR
If and only—two small words that kept repeating themselves again and again in Janet's thoughts, but it was too late to go back now—it was as if she were riding a giant tidal wave [Because she was.], it would be folly to fight against it—her only chance would be to ride it out—adapt—and perhaps also—survive.
(Enter ROCKY.)

ROCKY
Oh! Its you—look I'm trying to hide from my creator and his minion—they scare me—I feel that all is not well here. I have been thinking a lot about—*(Eddie)* I have a feeling of foreboding.
JANET
It's all like some terrible dream.

ROCKY
Is it true you don't like men with too many muscles?
JANET
Well . . .
ROCKY
Have you got any lip gloss?
JANET
I'm engaged to Brad, just the same as Betty Munroe was to Ralf Hapshatt. [Happ-shit!] But Frank's kisses overwhelmed me with an ecstasy I had never dreamed of before—hot burning kisses—I could see Brad's face before me, and my mind screamed—No!—but my lips were hungry, too hungry—I wanted to be loved, and loved completely—my body throbbed excitedly—Oh Brad, Brad my darling how could I have done this to you.
ROCKY
This room is a womb to me.
JANET
Yes—there you see, it's instinctive—you returned here for one thing—security. Oh where's Brad—? *(She fiddles with TV monitor.)* What have they done with him?

NARRATOR
Janet's feelings ran wild as she frantically manipulated the selector switch on the TV monitor—The screen threw up images of empty rooms and corridors—finally she stopped—at Frank's bedroom. *(Sees FRANK kissing BRAD.)*
JANET
Aaahhh!
NARRATOR
Aaahhh!
ROCKY
Oh, you can't rely on anyone.
JANET
Oh Brad!—How could you? [How could he? How could you?!]
(They all bend over trying to work out position on screen.)

NARRATOR
If one is suffering from the pangs of remorse for a sexual indiscretion—it would seem logical that the transgressor would be sympathetic toward a loved one caught committing a similar misdemeanor—But emotion is an irrational and powerful master—and from what Janet witnessed on the monitor [Eager beavers.]—there seemed little doubt that she was indeed its slave.

(MAGENTA and COLUMBIA enter and watch quietly.)
MAGENTA & COLUMBIA
Tell us about it, Janet.

TOUCH-A TOUCH-A TOUCH ME

JANET
I WAS FEELING DONE IN
COULDN'T WIN
I'D ONLY EVER KISSED BEFORE [You mean she went to BYU?]
MAGENTA & COLUMBIA
YOU MEAN SHE'D ONLY EVER KISSED
JANET
AHA
I THOUGHT THERE'S NO USE GETTING [Laid!]
INTO HEAVY PETTING
IT ONLY LEADS TO TROUBLE
AND SEAT WETTING
NOW ALL I WANT TO KNOW
IS HOW TO GO
I'VE TASTED BLOOD AND I WANT MORE.
MAGENTA & COLUMBIA
MORE, MORE, MORE
JANET
I'LL PUT UP NO RESISTANCE
I WANT TO STAY THE DISTANCE
I'VE GOT AN ITCH TO SCRATCH
AND I NEED ASSISTANCE
(CHORUS)
TOUCH-A TOUCH-A TOUCH-A-TOUCH ME
I WANT TO BE DIRTY
THRILL ME CHILL ME FULFILL ME
CREATURE OF THE NIGHT
THEN IF ANYTHING GROWS [It will!]
WHEN YOU POSE
I'LL OIL YOU UP AND RUB YOU DOWN
MAGENTA & COLUMBIA
[Up!] DOWN, [Up!] DOWN, [Up!] DOWN
AND THAT'S JUST ONE SMALL FRACTION
OF THE MAIN ATTRACTION
YOU NEED A FRIENDLY HAND
AND I NEED ACTION
JANET
TOUCH-A TOUCH-A TOUCH-A-TOUCH ME
I WANT TO BE DIRTY
THRILL ME CHILL ME FULFILL ME
CREATURE OF THE NIGHT
TOUCH-A TOUCH-A TOUCH-A-TOUCH ME
I WANT TO BE DIRTY
THRILL ME CHILL ME FULFILL ME
CREATURE OF THE NIGHT
TOUCH-A TOUCH-A TOUCH-A-TOUCH ME

I WANT TO BE DIRTY
THRILL ME CHILL ME FULFILL ME
CREATURE OF THE NIGHT
CREATURE OF THE NIGHT
CREATURE OF THE NIGHT
(Blackout)

Scene Eight

(RIFF RAFF enters fleeing from FRANK. He runs toward MAGENTA.)

RIFF RAFF
Aaaggghhh!—Mercy! Master
FRANK
(With whip.) How did it happen? [Beats me!]
I understood you were to be watching.
RIFF RAFF
I was only away for a moment, [Doing what?]
Master . . . [Bating!]
FRANK
See if you can find him on the monitor.
Oh Magenta. Oh Rocky. Oh Rocky. Oh Rocky.
(Click—BRAD's empty room—switch—switch—switch—JANET's room.)
RIFF RAFF
I've located him in the female's quarters, Master.
FRANK
Rocky! I think I'm going to . . . *(FRANK faints.)*
RIFF RAFF
Faint.
MAGENTA
Master.
(They laugh as they carry him off.)
BRAD
(Enters, sees TV.)
Janet! How could she? That's it—it's over.
NARRATOR
Over! What was over? Not the night that was certain. Brad and Janet's engagement? Their love for one another? Who could say—for questions such as these are not to be answered by the academic, they must be left for the heart to solve and Brad you may be sure, had plenty of heart.

ONCE IN A WHILE

BRAD
ONCE IN A WHILE
SHE DON'T WANT TO CALL YOU
SPEAKING ON THE TELEPHONE
AND ONCE IN YOUR LIFE
SHE DON'T WANT TO KNOW YOU
YOU LOOK AROUND
THE ONE YOU FOUND
SHE IS GONE
NARRATOR
HUMMINAH HUMMINAH HUMMINAH HUMMINAH HUM
BRAD
AND THAT'S ALL THE TIME
THAT IT TAKES
FOR A HEART TO TURN TO STONE
THE SWEETER THE WINE
THE HARDER TO MAKE THE BREAK
YOU HEAR SOMETHING
ABOUT SOMEONE YOU THOUGHT YOU'D KNOWN
SO BABY DON'T CRY
LIKE THERE'S NO TOMORROW
AFTER THE NIGHT THERE'S BRAND NEW DAY
AND THERE'LL BE NO PAIN
AND NO MORE SORROW
SO WASH YOUR FACE
AND PHONE MY PLACE. IT'LL BE OKAY
AND THAT'S ALL THE TIME
THAT IT TAKES
FOR A HEART TO BEAT AGAIN
SO GIVE ME A SIGN
THAT A LOVER MAKES
YOU LOOK AROUND THE ONE
FOUND IS BACK AGAIN . . . IS BACK AGAIN
(FRANK and RIFF RAFF enter.)
FRANK
How maudlin—how pathetic—Your baggage has dared to defile my beautiful creature—Oh Rocky how could you?
RIFF RAFF
(Fiddles with TV monitor.)
Master—we have a visitor. [It's Mary Poppins taking a shit!]
FRANK
Oh shit.
BRAD
Great Scott—Scotty—[Beam me up, this planet sucks!] Dr. Evrett Scott.
RIFF RAFF
You know this earth—
(FRANK stops RIFF RAFF.)
FRANK
This person.
BRAD
Yes, I do. He's an old friend of mine. [Assholes don't have friends, just hemorrhoids.]
FRANK
I see—so this wasn't simply a chance meeting—you came here with a purpose.
BRAD
That's not true—my car broke down—I told you.

FRANK

I know what you told me, Brad—but this Dr. Evrett Scott, his name is not unknown to me.

BRAD

He was a science teacher at Denton High.

FRANK

And now he works for your Government—doesn't he, Brad? He's attached to the bureau of the investigation of that which you call UFO's—that's right, isn't it, Brad?

BRAD

He might be—I don't know.

RIFF RAFF

The intruder is entering the building, Master.

FRANK

[Where could he be?] Ah he's in the Zen room. [Zen go get him!] Seal off all exits—and all doors—except for those that lead here—Riff Raff—bring Rocky and Janet here—I think we should make this a social occasion. The three unexpected guests shall entertain us with a floor show—which I shall direct.

(FRANK makes a signal and door opens revealing DR. SCOTT.)

Scene Nine

(Enter DOCTOR SCOTT in wheelchair—COLUMBIA pushing him.)

COLUMBIA

Hi—Ho—Silver.

BRAD

Dr. Scott!

SCOTTY

Brad—what are you doing here? [Oh, just fucking around.]

FRANK

Don't play games, Dr. Scott. It was part of your plan, was it not, that Brad Majors and his female should check the layout for you [Or lay the checkout!]—unfortunately for you all there is to be a change of plans [Who died and made you the director?]—I'm sure you're adaptable, Dr. Scott [AC/DC!]—I know Brad is. [You promised you wouldn't tell!]

SCOTTY

I can assure you that Brad's presence here comes as a complete surprise to me. [When Brad comes, it's always a surprise!] As does the set up you have here—I didn't expect it to be quite so . . .

(He goes to inspect laboratory.)

FRANK

Sophisticated—Dr. Scott? Or should I say Dr. Von Scott?

BRAD

What exactly are you implying?

SCOTTY

They didn't prove nothink! Ah—this machine here . . .

BRAD

What do you think it is, Doc?

SCOTTY

At this precise moment it's hard to tell—but it seems to be made of a metal that is not of this earth—I would say it was from another planet.

(JANET and ROCKY are revealed in lab.)

JANET

Brad! [Mouseketeer roll call sound off now!]

SCOTTY

Janet!

FRANK

Rocky! [Bullwinkle!]

JANET

Dr. Scott! Brad!

SCOTTY

Janet!

FRANK

Rocky! [Bullwinkle!]

JANET

Dr. Scott! Brad!

SCOTTY

Janet!

FRANK

Rocky! [Bullwinkle!]

JANET

Dr. Scott!

FRANK

Oh Rocky. [Bullwinkle!] Oh Rocky!

ROCKY

Piss off.

FRANK

Listen—I made him and I can break him just as easily—I'll pull his plug out.

SCOTTY

I suppose you intend to do with us as you did for Eddie.

PHANTOMS

Sshh!

COLUMBIA

Eddie!

MAGENTA & RIFF RAFF

Sshh!

BRAD

Eddie—I've seen him, he looks terrible.

PHANTOMS

Sshh!

FRANK

What do you know of Eddie, Dr. Scott?

SCOTTY

I happen to know a great deal about a lot of things [Do you know how to walk?]—you see Eddie happens to be my nephew.

BRAD

Dr. Scott!

SCOTTY

Yes, Brad—my sister's boy. I knew he was in with a bad crowd, but it was worse than I imagined—aliens.

BRAD

Tell them, Doc.

EDDIE'S TEDDY

SCOTTY

FROM THE DAY HE WAS BORN [Not the night, but the day.] HE WAS TROUBLE [With a capital T!]
HE WAS THE THORN [Not the rose, but the thorn!]
IN HIS MOTHER'S SIDE [Not the back, but the side!]
SHE TRIED IN VAIN

NARRATOR

BUT HE NEVER CAUSED HER NOTHING BUT PAIN

SCOTTY

HE LEFT HOME THE DAY SHE DIED EIN SWEI TREI
FROM THE DAY SHE WAS GONE
ALL HE WANTED
WAS A ROCKIN' ROLL PORN AND A MOTOR BIKE [vroom vroom!]
SHOOTIN' UP JUNK

NARRATOR

HE WAS A LOW DOWN CHEAP LITTLE PUNK [Yay punks!]

SCOTTY

TAKING EVERYONE FOR A RIDE [He never took me!]

ALL

WHEN EDDIE SAID HE DIDN'T LIKE HIS TEDDY
YOU KNEW HE WAS A NO GOOD KID [Oy-vey!]
BUT WHEN HE THREATENED YOUR LIFE
WITH A SWITCH BLADE KNIFE

FRANK

WHAT A GUY

COLUMBIA

MADE YOU CRY

SCOTTY

AND I DID

COLUMBIA

EVERYBODY SHOVED HIM
I VERY NEARLY LOVED HIM
I SAY HEY LISTEN TO ME
STAY SANE INSIDE INSANITY
BUT HE LOCKED THE DOOR AND THREW AWAY THE KEY

SCOTTY

BUT HE MUST HAVE BEEN DRAWN [With a pencil or pen?] INTO SOMETHING
MAKING HIM WARN ME IN A NOTE WHICH READ [What's it say, what's it say?]

ALL

WHAT'S IT SAY, WHAT'S IT SAY?

SCOTTY

I'M OUT OF MY HEAD

NARRATOR

HURRY OR I MAY BE DEAD

SCOTTY

THEY MUSTN'T CARRY OUT THEIR EVIL DEEDS

ALL

WHEN EDDIE SAID HE DIDN'T LIKE HIS TEDDY
YOU KNEW HE WAS A NO GOOD KID
BUT WHEN HE THREATENED YOUR LIFE
WITH A SWITCH BLADE KNIFE
WHEN EDDIE SAID HE DIDN'T LIKE HIS TEDDY
YOU KNEW HE WAS A NO GOOD KID
BUT WHEN HE THREATENED YOUR LIFE
WITH A SWITCH BLADE KNIFE

FRANK

WHAT A GUY

SCOTTY

MAKES YOU CRY

COLUMBIA

AND I DID

ALL

HEY HEY HEY

FRANK

WHAT A GUY

SCOTTY

MAKES YOU CRY

COLUMBIA

AND I DID

ALL

HEY HEY HEY

FRANK

WHAT A GUY

SCOTTY

MAKES YOU CRY

COLUMBIA

AND I DID

ALL

YEAH YEAH YEAH

FRANK

WHAT A GUY

COLUMBIA

MAKES YOU CRY

SCOTTY
AND SHE DID
ALL
YES SHE DID
SCOTTY & COLUMBIA
AND WE DID
ALL
YES WE DID
EDDIE
FRANK
Say a prayer for Eddie, I just defrosted him. (He pulls out a bag of blood and gore.) His destiny is in the bag.
BRAD
Why you . . .
FRANK
(Flicks a switch.) There, that should restrain you all. Magenta.
(He holds out the bag.)
MAGENTA
I'll put him down the waste disposal.
FRANK
Clever girl.
JANET
My feet—there's something wrong with my feet.
SCOTTY
My wheels! My God! I can't move my wheels.
BRAD
[My socks! I can't move my socks!] It's as if we're glued to the spot.
FRANK
You are, so quake with fear you tiny fools—O.K. it's startime—Riff Raff set the sonic transducer on program 8 secure all levels at zero—
MAGENTA
Relax.
SCOTTY
You won't find earth people quite the easy mark that you imagine—this sonic transducer! It is I suppose some type of audio vibratory physiomolecular transport device!
FRANK
You'd better believe it, baby.
BRAD
You mean . . . ? [A vibrator!]
SCOTTY
Yes, Brad—it's something we ourselves have been working on. [A working vibrator.] But it seems our friend here has found a way of perfecting it [A perfect vibrator!]—a device that is capable of breaking down solid matter [A broken vibrator.] and then projecting it through space and who knows, perhaps even time itself. [A COSMIC vibrator!]
JANET
You mean he's going to send us to another planet?

PLANET SCHMANET

[PREPARE YOUR SPONGE]
FRANK
PLANET-SHMANET JANET
TELL YOU ONCE
WON'T TELL YOU TWICE
YOU'D BETTER WISE UP JANET WEISS
Y'APPLE PIE
DON'T TASTE TOO NICE
YOU'D BETTER WISE UP JANET WEISS
I'VE LAID THE SEED
IT SHOULD BE ALL YOU NEED
YOU'RE AS SENSUAL
AS A PENCIL
WOUND UP LIKE AN 'E' OR FIRST STRING
WHEN WE MADE IT
DID JA HEAR A BELL RING?
Y'GOT A BLOCK
TAKE MY ADVICE
YOU'D BETTER WISE UP JANET WEISS
THE TRANSDUCER
WILL SEDUCE YAH
IT'S SOMETHING YOU'LL GET USED TO
A MENTAL MIND-FUCK CAN BE NICE
YOU'D BETTER WISE UP—JANET WEISS
YOU'D BETTER WISE UP
BUILD YOUR THIGHS UP
YOU'D BETTER WISE UP
NARRATOR
AND THEN SHE CRIES OUT [For . . . ?]
JANET
STOP!
FRANK
DON'T GET HOT AND FLUSTERED
USE A BIT OF MUSTARD
(FRANK signals MAGENTA who pulls switch and releases them as RIFF RAFF sprays them. COLUMBIA takes them off stage.)
ALL
YOU'RE A HOT DOG
BUT YOU'D BETTER NOT TRY TO HURT HER
FRANK FURTER
(BRAD is taken off by COLUMBIA.)
YOU'RE A HOT DOG
BUT YOU'D BETTER NOT TRY TO HURT HER
FRANK FURTER
(SCOTTY is taken off.)

YOU'RE A HOT DOG
BUT YOU'D BETTER NOT TRY TO HURT HER
FRANK FURTER
(JANET and ROCKY are taken off.)
YOU'RE A HOT DOG
BUT YOU'D BETTER NOT TRY TO HURT HER
FRANK FURTER

MAGENTA
(On her own.)
YOU'RE A HOT DOG
BUT YOU'D BETTER NOT TRY TO HURT HER
FRANK FURTER

FRANK
MAGENTA, RELAX
YOU'RE A HOT DOG
BUT YOU'D BETTER NOT TRY TO HURT HER
FRANK FURTER
(RIFF RAFF sprays her. She stops dramatically.)

FRANK
Columbia—the artistes are in a molecular state somewhere between entrance and exit. When they've pulled themselves together—see that they are prepared for the floorshow.
(COLUMBIA flips.)

COLUMBIA
My God! [Mine too!] I can't take any more of this. [Bitch bitch, nag nag!] First you ditch me for Eddie and then you throw him off like an old overcoat for Rocky. [He was heavy!] You chew people up and then you spit them out again. I loved you, do you hear? [What did you say?] I loved you, and what did I get? I'll tell you, a big fat nothing. [At least it was big!] You're like a sponge, [THROW YOUR SPONGE.] you take, take, take and drain others of their affection. Well, I've had it, I'm out of here, and I mean.
(RIFF RAFF sprays her.)
Oh wow—I dig that—it's wicked, it's a gas—I'm groovy I'm hip, man—it's like a trip—ah, wow, my God—freak out baby—dig you later.
(She exits.)

FRANK
It's not easy having a good time [try Disney-land!]—even smiling makes my face ache—and my children turn on me [Don't you mean "turn on you?"]—Rocky's behaving just as Eddie did—maybe I made a mistake in splitting his brain between the two of them.

MAGENTA
When do we return to Transylvania?—I grow weary of this world.

FRANK
Magenta I am indeed grateful to both you and your brother Riff Raff—you have both served me well—loyalty such as yours must be rewarded, and you will discover that when the mood takes me, I can be quite generous.

MAGENTA
I ask for nothing [Under twelve inches.], Master.

FRANK
And you shall receive it in abundance [Frank, what's your favorite high protein drink?]—come—our guests will be growing restless.
(FRANK exits. MAGENTA and RIFF RAFF look at one another—they make an extraterrestrial sign. Strobe light Blackout.)

NARRATOR
And so, by some extraordinary coincidence—fate it seems had decided that Brad and Janet should keep that appointment with their friend Dr. Evrett Scott. But, it was to be in a situation which none of them could have possibly foreseen—And, just a few hours after announcing their engagement Brad and Janet had both tasted [Frank's cock!] forbidden fruit [Same thing.]—This in itself was proof that their host was a man of little morals [Yay little morals!] and some persuasion [Gay persuasion]—What further indignities were they to be subjected to . . . ? And what of the sonic transducer and the floor-show that had been spoken of?—What indeed?—From what had gone before it was clear that this was to be [Can we have a picnic?] no picnic. [Aw.]

Scene Ten

(Each enters singly through slash curtain—wearing black stockings and suspenders and black underwear and finally they become a chorus line.)

FLOORSHOW / ROSE TINT MY WORLD
COLUMBIA
[How was this musical?] IT WAS GREAT
WHEN IT ALL BEGAN
I WAS A REGULAR FRANKY FAN
BUT IT WAS OVER WHEN HE HAD THE PLAN
TO START WORKING ON A MUSCLE-MAN
NOW THE ONLY THING THAT GIVES ME HOPE
IS MY LOVE OF A CERTAIN DOPE
ROSE TINTS MY WORLD KEEPS ME
SAFE FROM MY TROUBLE AND PAIN [How old are you?]
ROCKY

I'M JUST SEVEN HOURS OLD
TRULY BEAUTIFUL TO BEHOLD
AND SOMEBODY SHOULD BE TOLD
MY LIBIDO HASN'T BEEN CONTROLLED
NOW THE ONLY THING I'VE COME TO TRUST
IS AN ORGASMIC RUSH OF LUST
ROSE TINTS MY WORLD KEEPS ME
SAFE FROM MY TROUBLE AND PAIN [What's two plus two?]

BRAD

IT'S BEYOND ME
HELP ME MOMMY
I'LL BE GOOD YOU'LL SEE
TAKE THIS DREAM AWAY
WHAT'S THIS, LET'S SEE
I FEEL SEXY
WHAT'S COME OVER ME
HERE IT COMES AGAIN [How do you feel?]

JANET

I FEEL RELEASED
BAD TIMES DECEASED
MY CONFIDENCE HAS INCREASED
REALITY IS HERE
THE GAME HAS BEEN DISBANDED
MY MIND HAS BEEN EXPANDED
IT'S A GAS THAT FRANKY'S LANDED
HIS LUST IS SO SINCERE

FRANK

WHATEVER HAPPENED TO FAY WRAY [She jammed with King Kong!]
THAT DELICATE SATIN DRAPED FRAME
AS IT CLUNG TO HER THIGH
HOW I STARTED TO CRY [Why?]
FOR I WANTED TO BE DRESSED JUST THE SAME [But you are!]
GIVE YOURSELF OVER TO ABSOLUTE PLEASURE
SWIM THE WARM WATERS OF SINS OF THE FLESH
EROTIC NIGHTMARES BEYOND ANY MEASURE
AND SENSUAL DAYDREAMS TO TREASURE FOREVER—
CAN'T YOU JUST SEE IT
WHOA WHOA WHOA
(Spoken) Don't dream it—be it.
ALL *(Sung)*
DON'T DREAM IT—BE IT
DON'T DREAM IT—BE IT
DON'T DREAM IT—BE IT
DON'T DREAM IT—BE IT
DON'T DREAM IT—BE IT
DON'T DREAM IT—BE IT
DON'T DREAM IT—BE IT

SCOTTY

Hmm . . . We've got to get out of this trap
Before this decadence [Yay decadence!] saps our wills [Too late!]
I've got to be strong and try to hang on
Or my mind may well snap
And my life will be lived
(SCOTTY reveals stockings and high heels.)
(Sings)
FOR THE THRILLS

BRAD

IT'S BEYOND ME
HELP ME MOMMY

JANET

GOD BLESS LILY ST. CYR
FRANK
MY MY MY MY MY MY MY
MY MY MY MY MY MY MY
(They all form chorus line.)
I'M A WILD AND UNTAMED THING
I'M A BEE WITH A DEADLY STING
GET A HIT AND YOUR MIND GOES PING
YOUR HEART'LL THUMP
AND YOUR BLOOD WILL SING
SO LET THE PARTY AND THE SOUNDS ROCK ON
GONNA SHAKE IT TILL THE LIFE HAS GONE
ROSE TINT MY WORLD
KEEP ME SAFE FROM MY TROUBLE AND PAIN

ALL

WE'RE A WILD AND UNTAMED THING
WE ARE BEES WITH A DEADLY STING
GET A HIT AND YOUR MIND GOES PING
YOUR HEART'LL THUMP
AND YOUR BLOOD WILL SING
SO LET THE PARTY AND THE SOUNDS ROCK ON
GONNA SHAKE IT TILL THE LIFE HAS GONE
ROSE TINT MY WORLD
KEEP ME SAFE FROM MY TROUBLE AND PAIN
WE'RE A WILD AND UNTAMED THING
WE ARE BEES WITH A DEADLY STING
GET A HIT AND YOUR MIND GOES PING
YOUR HEART'LL THUMP
AND YOUR BLOOD WILL SING
SO LET THE PARTY AND THE SOUNDS ROCK ON
GONNA SHAKE IT TILL THE LIFE HAS GONE
ROSE TINT MY WORLD
KEEP ME SAFE FROM MY TROUBLE AND PAIN
(RIFF RAFF and MAGENTA enter dressed in e xtraterrestrial national costume.)

RIFF RAFF

FRANK N FURTER
IT'S ALL OVER
YOUR MISSION IS A FAILURE
YOUR LIFESTYLE'S TOO EXTREME

I'M YOUR NEW COMMANDER
YOU NOW ARE MY PRISONER
WE RETURN TO TRANSYLVANIA
PREPARE THE TRANSIT BEAM
(Song ends.)
(All freeze.)
FRANK
Wait [Can you explain?]—I can explain.

I'M GOING HOME

FRANK
ON THE DAY I WENT AWAY
ALL
GOODBYE
FRANK
WAS ALL I HAD TO SAY
ALL
NOW I
FRANK
WANT TO COME [so does Brad] AGAIN AND STAY
ALL
OH MY MY
FRANK
SMILE AND THAT WILL MEAN I MAY
I'VE SEEN BLUE SKIES
THROUGH THE TEARS IN MY EYES
AND I REALIZE I'M GOING HOME
ALL
I'M GOING HOME.
FRANK
EVERYWHERE IT'S BEEN THE SAME
ALL
FEELING
FRANK
LIKE I'M OUTSIDE IN THE RAIN
ALL
WHEELING
FRANK
FREE TO TRY AND FIND A GAME
ALL
DEALING
FRANK
CARDS FOR SORROW CARDS FOR PAIN
I'VE SEEN THE BLUE SKIES
THROUGH THE TEARS IN MY EYES
AND I REALIZE—I'M GOING HOME
ALL
I'M GOING HOME
I'M GOING HOME

Scene Eleven

MAGENTA
How sentimental. [You bitch!]
RIFF RAFF
And also presumptuous of you—[F!] you see [K!] when I said 'we' were to return I referred only to Magenta [Who's Magenta?] and myself—I'm sorry however if you found my words misleading—you see you are to remain here [In what metaphysical form?]—in spirit anyway—*(He produces a ray gun.)*
SCOTTY
Great heavens—that's a laser.
RIFF RAFF
Yes, Dr. Scott, a laser capable of emitting a beam of pure anti-matter. [Then it's not a laser!]
BRAD
You mean you're going to kill him? [Yep!]—What's his crime?
FRANK
Oh Brad.
SCOTTY
You saw what had become of Eddie—Society must be protected. [Society is fucked, look at us!]
RIFF RAFF
Exactly, Dr. Scott—Now Frank-N-Furter, your time has come—say goodbye to all this [Goodbye, all of this!]—and hello to oblivion. [Hi, oblivion! How's the wife and kids?]
FRANK
Do your worst—inferior one.
COLUMBIA
[A blink of the eye, a twitch of the lips, the first one to scream gets it right in the tits!]
No! No!
(COLUMBIA runs to shield FRANK, she is hit.)
[Nice shot!]
FRANK
Did you do this for me?
(COLUMBIA nods.)
Silly bitch.
(COLUMBIA dies.) [Oh my God, you killed Frank! You bastard!]
(FRANK is killed—he dies slowly. ROCKY is killed—RIFF has to hit him numerous times as ROCKY attempts to avenge FRANK's death.)
BRAD
Good God.
RIFF RAFF
Yes.

JANET
You've killed them. [Thanks, captain obvious!]
MAGENTA
I thought you liked them—they liked you.
RIFF RAFF
(Screams)
They didn't like me—They never liked me. You saw the way things were—the way they were going.
SCOTTY
You did right. *(RIFF RAFF points gun at SCOTTY.)* Oh shit.
RIFF RAFF
A decision has to be made.
SCOTTY
You're O.K. by me.
RIFF RAFF
Dr. Scott I'm sorry about your nephew.
SCOTTY
Yes—Perhaps it's for the best.
RIFF RAFF
You should leave now, Dr. Scott
While it is still possible
We are about to beam the entire house
Back to the planet of Transsexual [Where's that?]
MAGENTA
In the galaxy of Transylvania.
RIFF RAFF
Go now.
(BRAD, JANET and DR. SCOTT exit.)
SCOTTY
Janet, schnell . . . Brad.
RIFF RAFF
Our noble mission is almost completed my most beautiful sister, and soon we shall return to the Moon drenched shores of our beloved planet.
MAGENTA
Ah . . . Sweet Transsexual, Land of Night, to sing and dance once more to your dark refrain, to take that step . . . to the RIGHT.
(They do so.)
RIFF RAFF
But it's the pelvic thrust.
PHANTOMS
That really drives you insane.
(They prepare to leave.)
MAGENTA
And our world will do the Time Warp again.
RIFF RAFF
Activate the transit crystal.
(Explosion. Blackout.)

SUPER HEROES
BRAD
I'VE DONE A LOT
GOD KNOWS I'VE TRIED
TO FIND THE TRUTH
I'VE EVEN LIED
BUT ALL I KNOW
IS DOWN INSIDE
PHANTOMS
I'M BLEEDING
JANET
AND SUPER HEROES
COME TO FEAST
TO TASTE THE FLESH
NOT YET DECEASED
AND ALL I KNOW
IS STILL THE BEAST
PHANTOMS
IS FEEDING
AHHH AHHH
NARRATOR
AND CRAWLING ON [Where?] THE PLANET'S FACE
SOME INSECTS CALLED [What are they called?]
THE HUMAN RACE [Oh shit, that's us!]
LOST IN TIME
[What's your favorite science fiction TV show?]
AND LOST IN SPACE
PHANTOMS
AND MEANING
(Song ends.)

Epilogue
SCIENCE FICTION/DOUBLE FEATURE
USHERETTE
SCIENCE FICTION DOUBLE FEATURE
FRANK HAS BUILT AND LOST HIS CREATURE
DARKNESS HAS CONQUERED BRAD AND JANET
THE SERVANTS GONE TO A DISTANT PLANET
OH—AT THE LATE NIGHT DOUBLE FEATURE
PICTURE SHOW—I WANT TO GO—OHH—
TO THE LATE NIGHT DOUBLE FEATURE PICTURE SHOW
(MR. BASSMAN's voice.)
DO LANG DOO LANG
THE END
(Blackout)

Photo credits

Alamy: 26–27, 107, 123, 85; **Everett Collection:** 24, 28, 33, 34, 42, 89; **Getty Images:** *Evening Standard/ Stringer* 8, *Michael Ochs Archives/Stringer* 120; © **Interfishnet Ltd.:** 2, 45; **Mark Jabara:** 14, 16, 18, 38–39, 41, 46–47, 56–57, 58, 61, 62, 65, 66, 71, 72, 76, 79, 93, 97, 98–99, 103, 104, 110–111, 113, 114, 118–119, 126–27, 129, 152; **Tom Keller Photography:** 6; **Linus O'Brien:** 4, 20, 52, 150; **Photostage:** 49, 55, 65, 68.

weldon**owen**

an imprint of Insight Editions
P.O. Box 3088
San Rafael, CA 94912
www.weldonowen.com

CEO Raoul Goff
SVP Group Publisher Jeff McLaughlin
VP Publisher Roger Shaw
Executive Editor Karyn Gerhard
Editorial Assistant Jon Ellis
Managing Editor Michelle Hope
VP Creative Chrissy Kwasnik
Art Director Megan Sinead Bingham
VP Manufacturing Alix Nicholaeff
Production Manager Joshua Smith
Strategic Production Planner Lina s Palma-Temena

Design by Roger Gorman, Reiner Design Consultants, Inc.

Weldon Owen would also like to thank Sheri Linden and Lee Stokes for their work on this project.

Special thanks to Richard and Linus O'Brien, Adam Gibbs, Mark Jabara, Charlie Day, Rebeckah Dalton, and Roger Gorman, without whose guidance, expertise, and spirit of collaboration this book could not have been possible.

ISBN: 979-9-88674-335-7

Manufactured in China by Insight Editions
10 9 8 7 6 5 4 3 2 1

Insight Editions, in association with Roots of Peace, will plant two trees for each tree used in the manufacturing of this book. Roots of Peace is an internationally renowned humanitarian organization dedicated to eradicating land mines worldwide and converting war-torn lands into productive farms and wildlife habitats. Roots of Peace will plant two million fruit and nut trees in Afghanistan and provide farmers there with the skills and support necessary for sustainable land use.

THE ROCKY HORROR SHOW

ALIVE ON STAGE

Music Book & Lyrics by RICHARD O'BRIEN
Director JIM SHARMAN
Designer BRIAN THOMPSON Costumes SUE BLANE
Lighting GERRY JENKINSON Musical Arrangements RICHARD 'RITZ' HARTLEY
The Theatre Upstairs Production presented by MICHAEL WHITE

ALL SEATS BOOKABLE

CINEMA CHELSEA
148 KINGS ROAD SW3
BOX OFFICE 352 4388

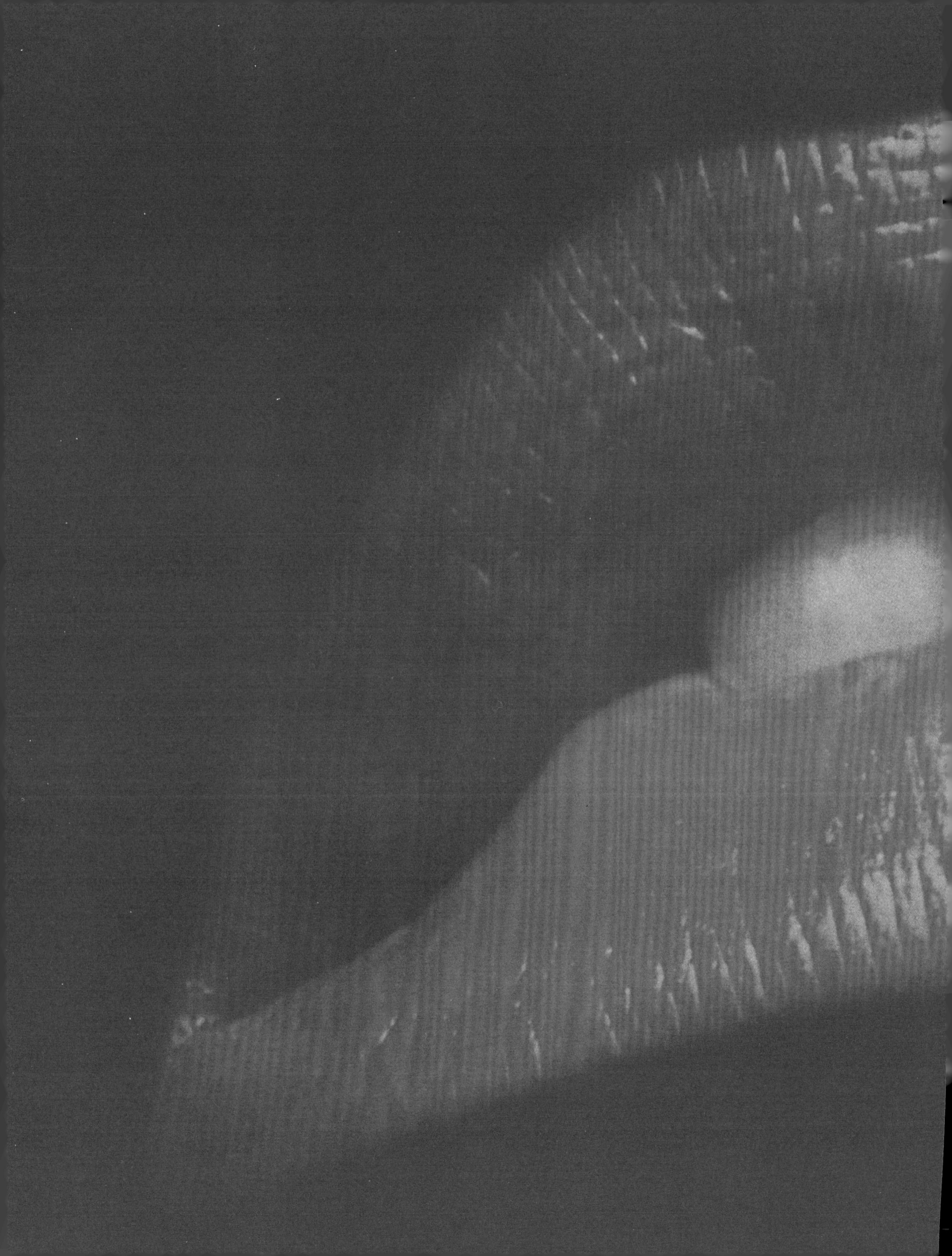